TIBET
A
LOST
WORLD

This exhibition and publication have been supported by grants from SCM Corporation and the National Endowment for the Arts. Their generous sponsorship is gratefully acknowledged.

It is fitting that this exhibition is titled "Tibet: A Lost World," since for centuries Tibet was hidden from the world by the towering peaks of the Himalayas. This isolation obscured a magnificent tradition of art and crafts that now comes alive as a result of the efforts of The Newark Museum and The American Federation of Arts. "Tibet: A Lost World" offers to thousands of people across the United States an opportunity to see for the first time one of the finest collections of Tibetan art in the world. The extensive scope of this exhibition, ranging from everyday objects such as saddles, costumes, jewelry and household utensils to exquisite works of Buddhist temple art, provides a rare insight into Tibetan life over four centuries. We at SCM Corporation are pleased to have played a role in this exhibition.

Paul H. Elicker, President
SCM Corporation

Vajravarahi, 17th-18th centuries, Cat. no. 199.

TIBET
A
LOST
WORLD

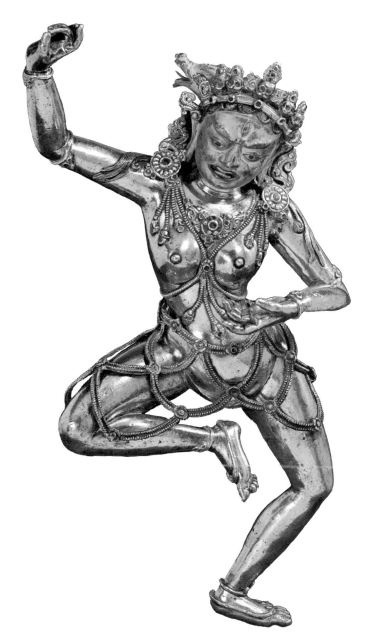

The Newark Museum Collection
of Tibetan Art and Ethnography

by Valrae Reynolds

The American Federation of Arts
New York

The American Federation of Arts is a national, non-profit, educational organization, founded in 1909, to broaden the knowledge and appreciation of the arts of the past and present. Its primary activities are the organization of exhibitions which travel throughout the United States and abroad, and the fostering of a better understanding among nations by the international exchange of art.

The Newark Museum was founded by John Cotton Dana in 1909 as a museum of art, science and industry. Its collections of American painting and sculpture and decorative arts are recognized nationally for their depth and quality and its collections of ancient glass and oriental art, especially objects from Tibet, are known and appreciated internationally.

© 1978 The American Federation of Arts
Published by The American Federation of Arts
41 East 65th Street
New York, New York 10021
Library of Congress Catalogue Number 78-66376
AFA Exhibition 77-1
Circulated November, 1978-December, 1979
Designed by Michael Shroyer
Type set by Haber Typographers, Inc. New York
Printing by The Arts Publisher, Inc., New York

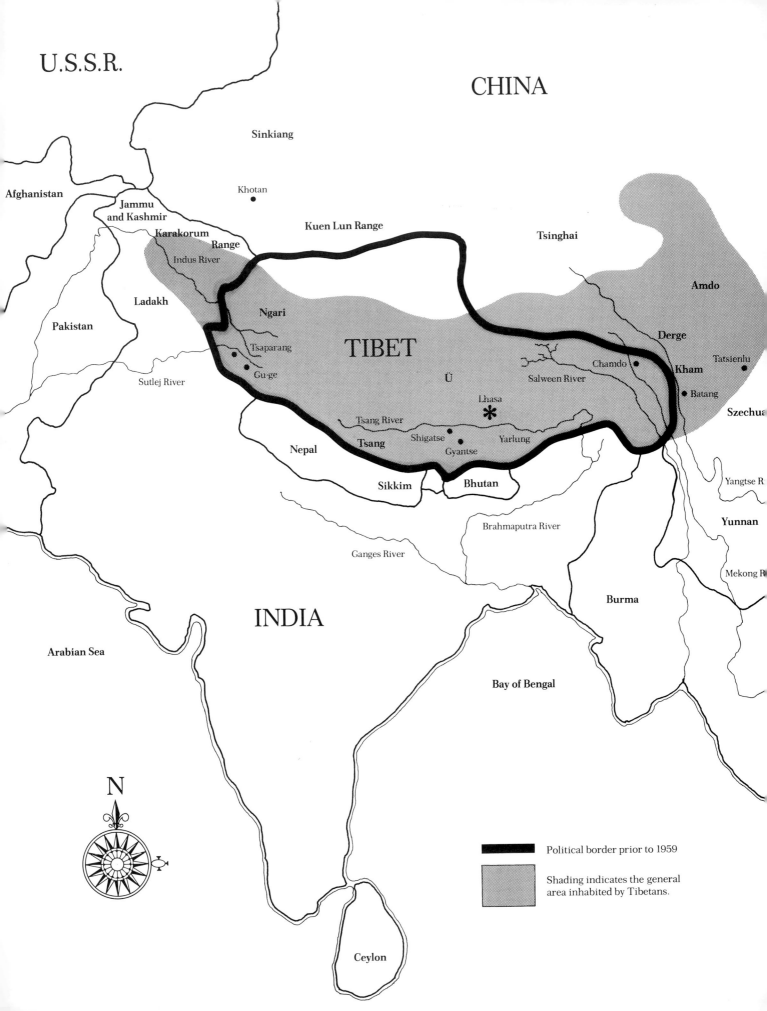

Contents

The Potala, Lhasa, during processions for the New Year's ceremonies. Giant appliqued banners are being unrolled on the front face.

Foreword

The phenomenon of Tibet, its spectacular geography, archaic life style, and religion have evoked a romantic response from the modern Western world. Thousands of Westerners are now studying with Tibetan Buddhist teachers and many more are at least superficially fascinated by the "shangra-la" aspects of this country closed off behind the Himalayas.

This unique civilization has been drastically altered during our own lifetime. The objects presented in this exhibition and catalogue, though originally collected to demonstrate the richness of a living culture, have now become artifacts of a "lost world" and the Buddhist-dominated society illustrated by the objects gathered here no longer exists.

This exhibition has been organized by The Newark Museum and The American Federation of Arts under the curatorial direction of Valrae Reynolds, Curator of Oriental Collections at the Museum, without whose energy and knowledge it could not have been accomplished. Audrey Koenig and Yuriko Grant of The Newark Museum staff have provided indispensable assistance in preparing material for the exhibition and catalogue. We extend to them our warmest thanks. We also wish to acknowledge with appreciation, Jane S. Tai, who coordinated all aspects of the exhibition at AFA, Michael Shroyer who skillfully designed this publication, Melissa Meighan who attentively cared for the objects while traveling, and Susanna D'Alton who arranged the exhibition's tour. Mary Ann Monet and Fran Falkin assiduously typed and proofread the manuscript at various stages.

Finally we would like to express our appreciation to SCM Corporation and to the National Endowment for the Arts for their generous grants, and to the museums across the country which will present the exhibition.

Samuel C. Miller, Director
The Newark Museum

Wilder Green, Director
The American Federation of Arts

Tibet and The Newark Museum

In December of 1910, on the steamship Mongolia en route from Yokohama to America, Edward N. Crane, a founding trustee of The Newark Museum, met Dr. Albert L. Shelton who was returning from a six-year mission in Western China and Eastern Tibet. As their shipboard friendship developed, Crane became interested in the group of Tibetan artifacts which Shelton had collected and wished to sell in order to finance the work of his mission hospital.

Albert L. Shelton, like most of the rare breed of men and women who ventured into Tibet in the 19th and early 20th centuries, seems to have been a person with unusual gifts. Born in Indianapolis in 1875, Shelton decided as a young man on the career of a medical missionary, obtained a medical degree and was sent to China in 1903 by the Foreign Christian Missionary Society, a group connected with the Disciples of Christ. He and his wife arrived in Tachienlu, a town in the mountain wilds of Sikang, Western China, in 1904. Although in political China, Tachienlu was on the edge of Kham, the Eastern Tibetan province then being rent by fierce fighting between Tibetan and Chinese forces. After four years and the birth of two daughters, the Sheltons moved their mission hospital west to the more completely Tibetan city of Batang. At that time Batang was just outside political Tibet but well into the Tibetan cultural area of Kham.

After the Sheltons arrived in the United States for their sabbatical, it was decided, at Crane's behest, that their approximately 150 items of Tibetan objects (paintings, images, books and domestic paraphernalia) would be lent to The Newark Museum for display. The hope was that they would be eventually purchased by the Museum. The fledgling institution in Newark was rather timid about purchasing 150 items from such an esoteric location as Tibet. When the Shelton items were put on view in Newark, however, the very exotic nature of the material seems to have made the exhibition a great success: from February to June, 1911, 17,724 people visited the display rooms. The matter of purchase was settled, in the end, when Crane suddenly died in the Summer of 1911. His wife and brother, in appreciation of Crane's interest in the collection, purchased it from Shelton and presented the entire lot to the Museum as a gift.

The Museum commissioned Dr. Shelton, upon his return to Batang in the Fall of 1913, to continue to collect Tibetan "curios" with the idea of adding to the Museum's original group. The difficulties of sending freight from Tibet to America are evident in a letter to the Museum from Shelton at this time, outlining the route and expenses:

> I'll give you as near I can the approximate cost, on 100 lbs. from Batang to New York.
>
> Freight
>
> | | |
> |---|---|
> | 460 miles on Yak (Batang to Tachienlu) about 8 Ru. | $2.00 |
> | 140 miles on men's backs to Yachow at 40 Cash about | 2.00 |
> | 600 miles by water to Ichang at about 30 Cash | 1.50 |
> | 1000 miles by steamer to Shanghai at 75¢ | .75 |
> | Shanghai to New York about | 3.50 |
> | | $9.75 |

Further letters in 1915 and 1916 refer to the precarious situation in the border areas. Despite the "war conditions," robbers and local rebellions mentioned in these letters, Shelton did manage to ship some items out in these intervening years. At that time only The American Museum of Natural History (New York) and the Field Museum (Chicago) had comparable Tibetan collections.

In late 1919, the Sheltons again left Batang for the United States, taking with them a large group of objects for The Newark Museum. In the vicinity of Yunnanfu, in the Chinese province south of Kham, twelve days out of Batang, their

The Jö Lama (center) with a nomad
family, Kham, ca. 1910.

Dr. Shelton, the Shelton daughters, the Jö Lama (between girls), and Tibetan nomads at a picnic, Kham, ca. 1910.

caravan was attacked by robbers. Dr. Shelton was taken captive and held for ransom; the rest of the party and most of the baggage escaped. Shelton was finally rescued in March of 1920 and returned with his family to the United States. The objects for the Museum, none the worse for the trip, arrived safely as well.

After a recuperative stay in America, Dr. Shelton returned to Batang. This time he was alone, Mrs. Shelton having gone to India to work on some translations, their two daughters remaining in the States for their schooling. Shelton intended to go on to Lhasa, Tibet's capital, and establish a medical mission there. He started out from Batang accompanied by the Prince of Batang, his teacher Gezong Ogdu, and some companions on February 15, 1922. One day out they received a note from the Governor of Mar Kham, asking them to turn back temporarily to Batang as the times were unfavorable for foreign visits to Tibet's interior. The next day, while heading back, Dr. Shelton was killed by bandits.

The Crane/Shelton collection, because of its known provenance and early date of acquisition, is a rich source of documentation for ritual as well as domestic objects. Amazingly diverse for a relatively provincial area, the pieces from the noble families and ruined monastery of Batang (many purchased with the assistance of Shelton's friends, the Jö Lama and the son of the Prince of Batang) are among the finest liturgical pieces ever to have left Tibet. The violent political climate provided the conditions under which an outsider such as Shelton could acquire these treasures.

Between 1928 and 1948 three more missionary collections, all from Northeastern Tibet were purchased, greatly enhancing the Museum's holdings of ethnographic and ceremonial art. These were the Robert Ekvall collection, from the Kokonor nomad region, Amdo, 1928, the Carter D. Holton collection, from Labrang, Amdo, 1936, and the Robert Roy Service collection, formed during trips to Northeastern Tibet and from Chinese traders in the border areas, 1948.

An important personality in the formation of the Museum's Tibetan archive was C. Suydam Cutting, a New York financier with estates in New Jersey. Cutting's expeditions to Tibet in 1935 and 1937 (he was the first American to visit Lhasa) were the result of his unique relationship with the 13th and 14th (present) Dalai Lamas. His memorabilia, now a part of the Museum collection, includes original manuscript correspondence with the Tibetan government, over 500 rare photographs, and silent films which are the earliest such documentation of the ceremonial life of Central Tibet.

The political events of the third quarter of the 20th century and the exodus of Tibetan people from their homeland have brought Tibetan artifacts into the commercial market in quantities unknown before 1959. Through gifts and purchases during the last 20 years, the Museum has been able to enrich its holdings of Central and Western Tibetan pieces. The scholarly assistance of Tibetan refugees in the New York, New Jersey area has allowed the Museum to greatly strengthen its research on the collection. Those who have helped particularly are Nima Dorjee, Lobsang Lhalungpa, Mr. and Mrs. Lobsang Samden, Tenzin Tethong, Mr. and Mrs. Phintso Thonden, and Dorjee Yuthok. Tsepon W. D. Shakabpa, on his several trips to the United States, has helped to catalogue the archive photographs and manuscripts.

Much of the research on the material included in this catalogue was done by Miss Eleanor Olson, Curator of the collection from 1938-1970 (in addition to being a curatorial assistant between 1930 and 1933). Most of the objects acquired before 1970 can be found in her five-volume catalogue of the collection. Prior to the arrival of Tibetan refugees in the New York area, Miss Olson was fortunate to have the kind assistance of Roderick A. MacLeod (Shelton's associate in Batang), Wesley E. Needham, and Schuyler V. R. Cammann for Tibetan translations.

Men with skin boat, Central Tibet, 1935.

Town of Gyantse with walled fortress in the background, *chorten* on left and bazaar in foreground, Southern Tibet, 1935.

The Physical Setting

The extravagant quality of the Tibetan environment has played a fundamental role in shaping the economics, religion, and art forms of the people. Tibet is vast and empty; situated on a high plateau of approximately one and a half million square miles with altitudes ranging from 4,000 to 20,000 feet. As the map indicates, "cultural Tibet" exceeded the boundaries of political Tibet, at least in the last 300 years. The barren nature of the North and West and the immense mountain ranges of the South (the Himalayas) and East have served as isolating barriers to Tibet's neighbors, developed and densely populated India and China. Pre-seventh century records on Tibet are scarce but there is evidence of ancient trading and cultural ties between the tribes of the central Tibetan valleys of Tsang, Ü, and Ngari with the Greco-Roman civilizations in the West (through passes into Khotan, Ladakh, and Kashmir) and with China to the East (through river valleys connecting to Sikang, Szechuan, and Yunnan). Tibetan armies in the 7th to 9th centuries and religious envoys in the 10th to 19th centuries maintained relations between the plateau and the vast plains of Central Asia to the North. Much of Tibet's material and spiritual heritage can be traced from the ancient connections with tribal Central Asia interacting with the sophisticated cultures of India and China.

Cultivated fields with Mt. Chomo Lhari
(23,930 ft.) in the distance, Southern
Tibet, 1935.

Prior to 1959, Tibetans lived in a manner unchanged since the Middle Ages. They had no electricity or mechanization, the economy was agricultural and nomadic. Valleys between 4,000 and 15,000 feet were cultivated for barley, wheat, oats, peas, nuts, and fruit. One half of the population was nomadic, moving in fixed routes from pasture to pasture with yaks, yak-cow hybrids, goats, sheep, and ponies as livestock. Despite the high altitude and dry climate, food was easily grown and herds could be fed where there was water and protection from the strong winds. The small population ($3\frac{1}{2}$ to 4 million) could easily support itself in a primitive but adequate standard of living.

Tibetans, spread across the isolated reaches of the plateau, were commonly united by their faith and language, both imported from India in the 7th century A.D. The unique Tibetan form of Buddhism, molded over the succeeding centuries by indigenous beliefs and new influxes of mystical practices and monastic reforms from the border regions, had become a state religion by the 11th century. Although separated from one another by great distances, the Tibetan people saw themselves unified as "people of the Faith," holding a common view of the supernatural as well as the earthly world.

To reach neighboring towns or to trade with China and India, Tibetans had to walk or ride yaks, mules, or horses. Such trips involved long lonely stretches with treacherous river crossings and high mountain passes which could be suddenly blocked by snow or rent by fierce winds. There were no wheeled vehicles and roads were rough and poorly maintained trails. Rivers were bridged when possible with crude cantilevered plank or rope suspension constructions, liable to wash out during the late summer monsoons. Wide and slow rivers were crossed in yak skin boats which had primitive steering systems and could only move with the current.

The Tibetan environment was not all lonely and bleak, however. The nomadic nature of the early Tibetans was from the first tempered by agricultural settlements in the fertile valleys. Tibetan and Chinese sources in the 7th and 8th century describe Tibet as a land ruled by small kingdoms already firmly entrenched in valley strongholds protected by forts and castles. The earliest extant architectural remains are tall stone towers and fortress palaces erected by the kings of the Yarlung valley in Central Tibet in the 7th century. Beautifully adjusted to the rocky quality of the land, Tibetan architecture, whether in humble farmhouses, fine manors, or monasteries, was in organic harmony to the landscape. Like the cliffs and mountains, the buildings had a massive and formidable presence. The characteristic inward sloping walls, stone or mud-brick construction and flat roofs gave the architecture a monumentality as well as a practical sturdiness. Isolated farmhouses gave families and herds (kept in the lower levels) protection from strong winds, extremes of temperatures, and marauders. On rock escarpments dominating a town or trading route, forts and monasteries provided psychological defense against potential enemies. The Potala in Lhasa, built between 1645 and 1695 (with some later additions), was the ultimate fortress in Tibet. The home of the Dalai Lama, the Potala, towered over Lhasa and served as an over-powering architectural entity reflecting its resident's control of both church and state.

The stark strength of the architecture was relieved by the colorful and gay painted decorations on the wood trim of windows, doors, and lintels. If possible, all such surfaces were densely covered with designs of Buddhist emblems, flowers, and folk tales. This light touch was further enhanced during festivals and holidays when private homes and monasteries were decked with awnings, banners, and flowers.

Tibetan farm houses, Kham, ca. 1910.

Tibetan nomads along the trail following the Mekong River, Kham, ca. 1910.

Amdo men assembled for a formal portrait, ca. 1930.

Group of men with their horses, Amdo, ca. 1930.

Nomads of Eastern Tibet

The nomads of Eastern Tibet, so well represented in Newark's collection, displayed many characteristics peculiar to their specific region but were typical of nomads throughout Tibet in their pastoral economy, dress, and domestic possessions. The rugged nomad maintained a centuries-old rhythm of life, moving easily with the seasons, driving their herds or trading loads of hide, fur, wool, salt, and coral to China in exchange for tea, silk, and silver. Assembled in extended families or tribal units of several hundred members, the nomads lived in large black yak-hair tents, held taut by numerous ropes and poles to withstand the fierce winds of the plateau. All possessions were made to be packed up and tied onto animals or to be worn on the nomad's bodies. Because of their situation in the border between Tibet proper and China, the clothes, jewelry, domestic objects, and weapons of the nomads show a mixture of Central Asian, Chinese, and Tibetan styles and motifs. As in ancient times, these tribal peoples in the 20th century took advantage of silks, silver, and iron from China, gemstones from Central Asia, amber from Burma, coral from the Mediterranean (by way of Central Asia), and European hats from India, bartering their own fur, wool, and dairy products for these desirable imports.

Starting with the basic *chupa,* the Tibetan version of the full-length robe worn throughout Northern and Eastern Asia, the nomads added their own particular decoration and jewelry to gain a distinctive local effect. The headdresses of Tibetan women varied greatly from area to area, even tribe to tribe, and served both as emblems of identity and as the family's "movable bank" of negotiable coins, silver, gems, and silks. The poorer nomads might have only a single sheepskin *chupa,* fur turned to their skin, worn trailing off the waist by both men and women on hot summer days. Wealthier nomads had silk and cotton undergarments and *chupas* of *pulu* (a fine native wool cloth) or imported cloth, trimmed with decorative banding and exotic furs. The *chupa* was worn by all Tibetans wrapped tightly around their waist and secured with a belt or sash. Excess cloth was pleated or bunched to the back and pouched over above the belt, sleeves extended well beyond the hand for warmth and were rolled up while working. Nomad men liked to affect a rakish air with the rope pulled up high and the right sleeve thrown off. This also enabled them freedom of movement, especially for riding.

The nomad was a formidable spectacle, bristling with weapons and ready for action. All objects pertinent to his daily business were strung on his body or stowed in the pouch of his *chupa.* The primitive matchlock gun was in general use in Tibet between the 16th century and 1904 when the British introduced rifles; Eastern nomads, however, continued to use the matchlock until 1959. It was carried as protection against brigands and to shoot game. The wicked-looking prongs at the tip folded down to serve as gun rests while firing from a kneeling position. Swords, tied on or thrust through the belt, were used for fighting, carving, and even digging. Bows and arrows were the ancient weapon of Tibet, used in the 20th century in lieu of or alongside guns for protection, as well as for hunting and in archery contests. Whips were carried for riding and herding. All these weapons reflected the social and financial position of their owners and were finely crafted and inlaid with precious substances when possible. Of equal importance to these weapons, for protection on the road, were boxes or small shrines containing prayers, charms, and various items to propitiate malignant spirits. Men wore large shrines strapped around their bodies and women had jewel-like boxes as neck ornaments. Living in an isolated and threatening world, Tibetans had a practical and aggressive attitude toward all dangers, both physical and spiritual, and armed themselves accordingly.

Domestic paraphernalia was compact and portable and formed from the richest materials the family could afford. Eating sets, after Chinese and Mongol custom, were carried at the belt by men and women. Flint and tinder pouches, necessary for starting campfires, were tied to the belt. Stored in the family tents was the equipment necessary for preparing and serving tea, beer, *tsamba* (a staple of the diet made of parched and ground barley), cheese, butter, yogurt, and meat.[1] These domestic utensils, though for mundane purposes, show the Tibetans' love of fine woods and metals and use of decorative design to enrich surfaces.

Man and child, Amdo, ca. 1930.

Nomadic existence led to the imaginative use of many forms of flat textiles, for bedding, seats, walls and decorative effects. Imported Chinese silk and cotton cloth was cut and sewn into garments, saddle pads, and many domestic objects. Felts and woolen cloth were made locally. Polychrome striping and tie-dyed circles and crosses were popular designs for wool. Narrow widths of striped wool or imported silk were woven by women and used as belts, garters, and trim.

[1] Most Tibetans were meat-eaters from nomadic custom and necessity (grains and vegetables were available only part of the year in some areas) although Buddhist doctrine forbids the killing of animals for food.

Note: All objects illustrated in this section were made in Tibet and date from the 19th and 20th centuries unless otherwise noted.

Nomad tent, Southern Tibet, 1935.

MILK PAIL HOOK
The rope handle to a milk pail was put around such a hook, worn suspended from the waist, during milking. For women who had servants to do this chore, the hook was worn as an ornament. This hook certainly has the appearance of a fine piece of jewelry rather than a practical implement. Silver medallions enclose turquoise and imitation coral stones and are set on an incised brass base. *Cat. no. 37.*

COVERED PAIL
Covered pails or buckets were practical items on a Tibetan farm or at a nomad encampment. They were used for storing and carrying water, milk, or beer. This nicely designed example has a copper body decorated with incised brass bands and interlace medallions, and a lotusform knob top. It is probably from the same owner as the teapot, p. 37. *Cat. no. 52a & b.*

QUIVER WITH ARROWS AND WHISTLING ARROW

Made in Kham, this fine wood quiver is covered in wool cloth and banded in chased silver. It was worn suspended by a leather strap from the waist. The arrows it held are of simple bamboo and feather construction with iron points. The "whistling" arrow also has a bamboo shaft with feather ends but the head is a hollow wood knob with perforations. Air rushing through the head created a whistle when these arrows were shot; they were used in archery contests and to scare up game. *Cat. nos. 47 & 48.*

WOMAN

Although she led a less vigorous life than her male counterpart, the nomad woman of Kham and Amdo required warm and flexible clothing. Identical in cut to the man's *chupa*, the woman's could be more lavish in material and was worn almost floor-length. Here, the inner robe is of native sheepskin, worn against the body, but lined with imported Chinese sateen. The thin outer robe is made of imported Chinese silk brocade with fine otter fur trim. The woman has thrown off part of her robe to show a handsome silk brocade jacket, also lined with fur. Like the nomad man, the woman needed free hands for her farming and cooking chores and wore necessary implements, such as eating sets, tied to her waist or tucked inside her robe. The eating set and chatelaine shown here were assembled in Tibet from imported Chinese brocades, silver, steel, and ivory. The most spectacular part of her ensemble is the massive headdress whose great weight is born jointly by the cotton and lambskin hat and by her own hair (here a wig) carefully formed into the auspicious 108 braids. Safely worn at all times on her body, yet comprised of easily dismantled and negotiable pieces, the headdress is in the particular style of one area of Amdo, thus proclaiming the woman's tribal identity (and the wealth and identity of her family). Local silver work with amber and coral beads, sewn onto a cloth backing, form part of the design. The large silver coins attached to the lower section show the sort of money available in Amdo in the early 20th century: regular Chinese government issue as well as Imperial mint issue for the various Chinese provinces; three are British trade dollars minted in India and distributed through Shanghai (and other ports). The coins date from the 1890's through the 1930's. *Cat. nos. 21-28.*

MAN'S HAIR ORNAMENT

Another example of Eastern Tibetan filigree silver work, here set with imitation coral beads, this hair ornament was tied to a silk or cotton scarf. Tibetan men in Amdo and Kham liked to affect dramatic hairstyles with elaborate braids and heavy jewelry. This ornament was worn at a sharp angle over one eye. See also p. 34. *Cat. no. 35.*

WOMAN'S HAIR ORNAMENT

This silver, coral, and turquoise pin was worn on a braid above the right eye by women of the Chiarong, Mantzu tribe in the Chinese-Tibetan borderlands. The image of the magical bird-god *garuda* (borrowed from Hindu mythology) is a protection against the diseases sent by the serpent demons. *Cat. no. 36.*

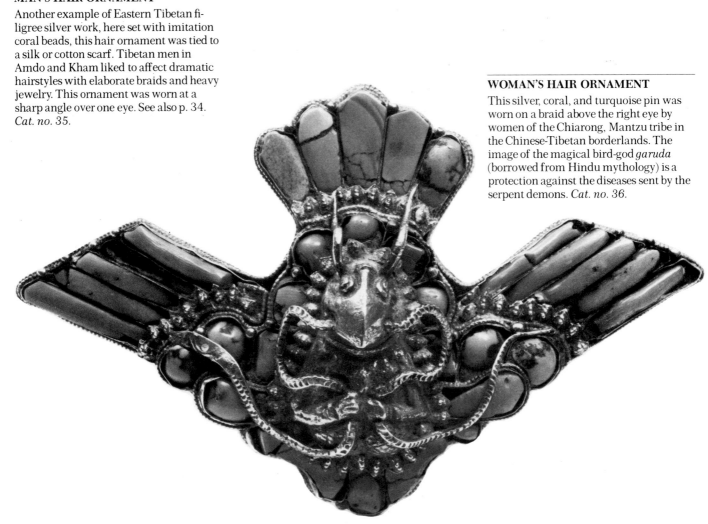

GROUP OF EARRINGS, ORNAMENTS, AND RINGS

Fine examples of Amdo and Kham silver work, this jewelry was the sort which adorned Tibetan men and women of the nomad and farmer status. The pair of women's earrings at left are cast in the shape of opposed dragons (facing a coral bead); the stylized form of these mythical beasts recalls Central Asian "animal style" bronzes. The beaded pendants, set with imitation coral, are another style of women's earrings. At center is a circular hairpin formed of beaded wire around a turquoise stone; this was worn by an Amdo woman. The single pendant earring, set with imitation coral, was worn by an Amdo man (most Tibetan laymen wore a single earring). At right are three types of finger rings, the two below set with turquoise and the "saddle ring" above with coral. Both types of rings were also worn as hair ornaments. *Cat. nos. 39-45.*

MAN WITH GUN

The assemblage of garments and equipment shown here, characteristic of the nomads of Amdo, reflect the availability of native and imported goods in Northeastern Tibet. The *chupa* is Chinese cotton sateen lined with local sheepskin and trimmed with imported silk stitching and other fur. The inner robe, exposed by the thrown off right sleeve, is of fine native *pulu* wool, trimmed in the woven stripe and tie-dyed wool made by Amdo women. The soft dome-shaped hat is of Chinese silk with fox fur trim. The long braid imitates a nomad man's own hair style, fastened with cotton cord and decorated with a piece of conch shell. The Mongolian style boots combine Russian and native leathers with Chinese silk and cotton cord trim.

The nomad's finely decorated weapons include an iron sword (from China or India) in a sheath made locally, decorated with silver repoussé and coral inlay, and a matchlock gun of imported iron and native silver, brass, bone and leather; the two-pronged fork on the gun is of antelope horn and wood. Powder is kept in the leather waist pouch decorated with brass and turquoise. Personal equipment for eating includes a handy sheath holding a knife and chopsticks (all of Chinese manufacture) tied at the waist, and a small wood bowl, kept inside the *chupa*. Of no less importance was the shrine strapped to the body providing spiritual protection on the road. *Cat. nos. 10-20.*

SNUFF HORN AND SNUFF BOTTLE

As in China, snuff (tobacco mixed with ash) was a popular substance in Tibet, taken by men and women of all classes throughout the country. The tobacco was imported primarily from India, dried and mixed with the ash, according to taste, by the user and stored in decorative containers. Yak horn and wood burl containers were the native Tibetan receptacles, often highly decorated and valuable possessions, prized in their own right (as were jade and glass snuff bottles in China). The horn shown here is mounted in silver decorated with a dragon design and inset coral and turquoise stones. The round burl box also has silver mountings of floral designs, set with imitation coral. *Cat. nos. 57 & 58.*

MAN WITH SWORD

The nomad of Northeastern (Amdo) and Eastern (Kham) Tibet attired himself with the garments and paraphernalia necessary in a cold and hostile environment. The heavy skin *chupa* provided warmth and great flexibility of movement. In the copious space inside the chest closing or thrust through and tied to the waist sash were stowed the objects needed for a day's ride or a lengthy expedition. Guns (with powder horn, chargers, and bullets) and swords were used for protection and hunting. The all-important flint and tinder pouch was the Tibetan form of portable match: the pouch contained a piece of flint and bit of soot and leaves or cotton; when struck against the steel bar at the base of the pouch, a spark was created which would be quickly transferred to a campfire or fuse. *Cat. nos. 1–9.*

SWORD AND SCABBARD

The pride which went into personal weapons is evident in this handsome sword and scabbard. The iron blade was probably imported from China or India but the chased designs and silver work of the hilt and scabbard are typical Eastern Tibetan work. Raised silver caps enclosing large turquoise and coral stones further attest to the wealth of the owner. *Cat. no. 46a & b.*

CHARMBOX

The fine silver filigree work and circular shape of this charmbox are typical of Eastern Tibetan work. The piece is further enriched by inset coral and turquoise stones. Charms (prayers, amulets, and images) were enclosed in the box, which was then worn strung on a beaded necklace by women of the Amdo region. For other types of charmboxes, see the one worn by the noble woman, p. 48 and the one on p. 62. *Cat. no. 34.*

TEAPOT

The squat robust shape of this teapot is the Tibetan variant of the spouted ewer found throughout Western and Eastern Asia. Of the sort used in a simple farmhouse or tent, the pot is made of fine wood burl, polished through years of use, mounted with brass interlace medallions. The lid is surmounted by a simple lotus-form knob. *Cat. no. 50.*

Two *Yasor* officials with attendants during the New Year's festival, Lhasa.

The Lhasa Nobility

Living in grand houses with a rather sedentary life style, the urban nobility of Tibet's capital, Lhasa, seems to sharply contrast with the nomads. Ennoblement could occur through descent from one of the ancient kings or chiefs of a local area (such as Yarlung, Gu-ge, or Kham), or from the families of the Dalai Lamas (many of whom were originally nomads or farmers). Ennoblement could also be attained by performing some service to the government. The nobility derived their wealth from ownership of land, often at some distance from Lhasa, and their power from membership in the government. All noble families sent sons into the clergy where they could rise to positions of importance in the theocracy, or into the civil service where they, similarly, could become lay officials. Daughters were married into other noble families to insure that estates were not split and weakened and that there were ample descendants.[1]

Although they maintained houses in Lhasa, to be close to the social and political life of the capital, most noble families spent considerable time managing their provincial estates. Lay or monk officials were also posted in outlying towns or monasteries. This small group of families thus had wide-ranging influence outside Lhasa. Like all tribal groups, the nobility retained the dress specific to their original home even when residing in other areas.

The Lhasa version of the *chupa* was made of fine silk from China, worn floor length with sleeves extended by both men and women. Women wore star-shaped charmboxes on fine jeweled necklaces and elaborate beaded bands at their chest. The characteristic Y-shaped headdress was sewn with pearls and corals of size and quality in accordance to the families' wealth. The large turquoise and pearl earrings were attached to the hair (augmented by a wig) to carry their great weight. Like a well-to-do nomad woman, a Lhasa noble lady displayed the family wealth on her body and favored imported luxury goods. The Lhasa noble gentleman, leading a sedentary life, presented quite a different spectacle from the nomad but, just as the latter bristled with weapons as an expression of his life style, the urban man wore jewelry and carried objects such as pen cases and seals, symbols of his duties and importance.

The nobility lived in handsome houses both in the capital and on their provincial estates, but like all Tibetans, also felt at home in a tent. The gay appliqued summer tent, pp. 42-43, is typical of the sort of "fair weather" tent used all over Tibet for festival days and picnics. Intended for religious as well as frivolous occasions, the tents were appliqued with protective emblems. Household possessions reflected the wealth and sophistication of the Lhasa upper class and included fine metal, porcelain, and ivory objects from China, India, and Nepal as well as from Lhasa and provincial Tibet. Like the nomads, the nobility were stylish travelers and loved to have their yaks and horses outfitted with the best saddles and trappings. Fine Derge saddles, such as the ones on p. 51 were much prized in Lhasa.

---

[1] If necessary, all the daughters of one family would marry one man, or one daughter could take several husbands. Marriage arrangements were primarily a matter of acquiring and retaining power and property. The situation of Tibetan women, however, was for Asia one of comparative freedom and independence. This was true for women of the nomad and farming classes as well as of the nobility.

Note: All objects illustrated in this section were made in Tibet and date from the 19th and 20th centuries unless otherwise noted.

The King of Derge with his two wives, son and attendants pose with a *tanka* and offering table. Note the Western-style clock on the table, Derge, Kham, ca. 1917.

Appliqued Tent, detail

APPLIQUED TENT FOR SUMMER OUTINGS

Used for picnics and official entertainments (which could last several days in Tibet) and to shelter the family during encampments at the great annual religious festivals, such gay "fair weather" tents were owned by all members of the nobility. The cotton fabric was imported from India but the applique work is typical of Lhasa. The decoration is meant to be pleasing and colorful, comprised of motifs which have religious significance; on the two sides of the roof is a *garuda* with serpents coiling from his beak, an Indian celestial spirit offering protection from disease, flanked by the Chinese celestial dragon. The phoenix, another Chinese heavenly creature, decorates the triangular roof ends. On the four walls of the tent are the eight Glorious Buddhist Emblems with the auspicious lion and tiger on the door flap. *Cat. no. 64.*

OFFICIAL'S SUMMER COSTUME AND HAT FINIAL

Once the official summer attire of *Tsepon* (Finance Minister) Shakabpa, this golden yellow Chinese silk robe shows the Lhasa style elegance of the native Tibetan *chupa*. This color, related both to the imperial yellow of China and the dark gold of the Tibetan clergy, was restricted to lay government officials. The dome-shaped yellow and gold brocade hat with long streamers is also a sign of office.

Shown separately is the *shalok* finial which would be attached to the hat. Also from Shakabpa's collection, it is a fine example of Lhasa gold filigree work, fashioned in the shape of the Buddhist vase of life. Cascading "water" of pearls and glass stones extend from the top over the spherical center of the "vase." The turquoise stone at the apex is the mark of the third government rank. Officials such as Shakabpa would wear the *shalok* and gold costume for all ceremonial occasions during the summer season in Lhasa. *Cat. nos. 66-69.*

OFFICIAL'S EARRINGS

A Lhasa lay government official (see p. 44) would wear this style earring as a mark of rank. This example is from the collection of Tashi Tshering. The long pendant, constructed to turquoise plaques on a gold granular base ending in a pointed glass bead, is worn in the left ear. The turquoise and pearl, strung on a cord, are worn in the right ear. *Cat. no. 84a & b.*

OFFICIAL'S CEREMONIAL ROBE

This magnificent ensemble, identical to the two central robes in the photograph on pp. 38-39, was last worn in office by Tethong Gyurmi Gyatso (1884-1938) who was a Shapé (lay minister of the Lhasa government) from 1932-5. Shapés wore these fur trimmed robes (T. *Kha Kha Su*) on the first day of the Tibetan New Year, for important government winter occasions, and in the annual *Yasor* ceremony (on the 23-24th days of New Year). Russian brocade seems to have been especially priced for its heavy sumptuous quality, combined here with silks imported from China, beaver and otter fur. The Persian sash may be as old as 18th century. *Cat. nos. 70-73.*

BRACELET AND MAN'S EARRING

Fine silver work is associated with Eastern Tibet but was also made and worn in Central Tibet. The handsome woman's bracelet is set with turquoise chips. The earring is the sort worn in the left ear by laymen of the Lhasa area who were not of government rank but who had sufficient means to attire themselves in an elegant manner. The turquoise stones set in beaded silver caps are particularly fine examples. *Cat. nos. 86 & 87.*

NOBLE WOMAN

A married woman from one of the noble families of Lhasa, ca. 1940, would have attired herself as shown here for social engagements. The brilliant magenta satin and black cut-velvet *chupa* is made from Chinese cloth and worn floor-length. The *chupa* is from the collection of the present Dalai Lama's elder sister. The multi-colored apron made of three lengths of native striped wool cloth is traditional for women of Central and Southern Tibet. The Y-shaped headdress marks the wearer as a resident of Lhasa; the size and number of the corals, pearls, and turquoises would be determined by the wealth of the

woman's family. The headdress (a replica) is attached to a specially constructed "horn"-shaped structure incorporating the woman's own hair and a wig; the hair is intertwined with pearls and corals in two tassels which trail off the back. Also attached to the headdress-wig are the heavy earrings of turquoise and pearls, set in a three medallion form typical of Lhasa. The ensemble is completed by a star-shaped silver, gold and turquoise charm-box strung on a coral and turquoise neck-lace and by an amber, mother-of-pearl, coral, and turquoise chest ornament. *Cat. nos. 74-80.*

PEN CASE

The pen case, a mark of status, would hold wooden sticks for writing letters and documents and was worn suspended from or thrust through the belt. This example is made of delicately cast iron decorated with an openwork design of dragons and deer amidst foliage, in front, with an incised pattern of overlapping scales and three *shou* emblems, in back. It was once completely gilded and now shows traces of gold. *Cat. no. 90.*

SEALS AND WAX

Any person of status, and all officials, used seals to sign letters and documents, a custom imported from China. Black ink (lamp black) was commonly used. Wax (boiled cowskin or lac) with a seal impression was employed to mark envelopes, packages, and important possessions. *Cat. no. 88.*

COFFER

The decoration on this handsome gilt copper box combines both Hindu and Buddhist iconography. This and the style of the workmanship suggest it was made in Nepal (where Hinduism and Buddhism flourish side by side), perhaps in the 18th century, and imported to Central Tibet. Of Hindu origin is the 18-armed goddess Durga with her lion fighting the demon-buffalo in a roundel on the hinged central lid. The sides have Buddhist deities and monks in quatrefoils. Common to both religions are the guardians and auspicious symbols along the border of the top. A similar box in the collection of the Rijksmuseum voor Volkenkunde, Leiden, was obtained on the Younghusband expedition (British, 1904) in Gyantse, Southern Tibet, perhaps from the Palkhor Choide Monastery (see p. 56). Such coffers were used to store valuables and ritual objects and were owned by high-ranking lamas or noble families. *Cat. no. 92.*

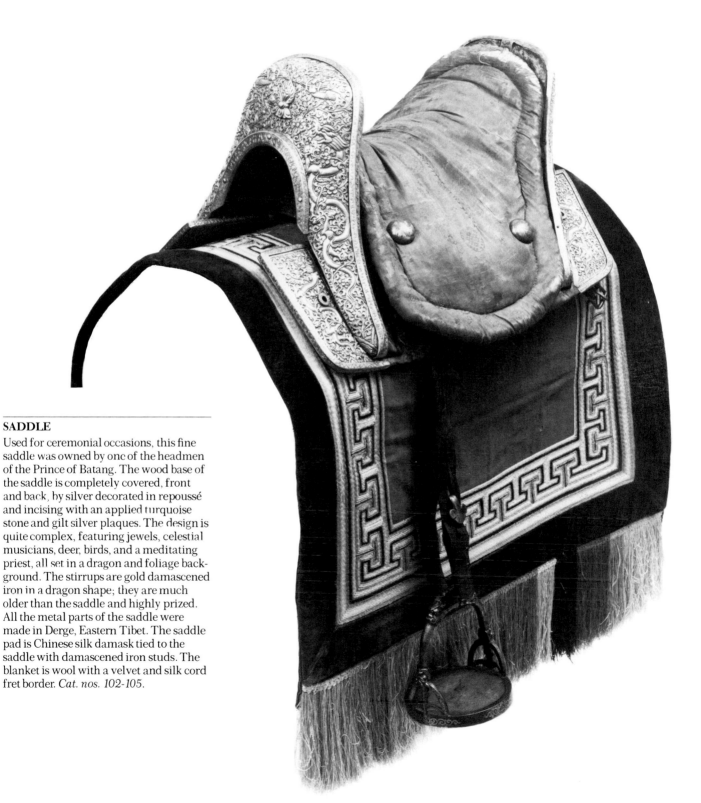

SADDLE

Used for ceremonial occasions, this fine saddle was owned by one of the headmen of the Prince of Batang. The wood base of the saddle is completely covered, front and back, by silver decorated in repoussé and incising with an applied turquoise stone and gilt silver plaques. The design is quite complex, featuring jewels, celestial musicians, deer, birds, and a meditating priest, all set in a dragon and foliage background. The stirrups are gold damascened iron in a dragon shape; they are much older than the saddle and highly prized. All the metal parts of the saddle were made in Derge, Eastern Tibet. The saddle pad is Chinese silk damask tied to the saddle with damascened iron studs. The blanket is wool with a velvet and silk cord fret border. *Cat. nos. 102-105.*

BEER JUG

Made in the famous metalworking center of Chamdo, Eastern Tibet, this beer jug is an elegant object which still retains the shape and material of its nomadic prototype. The flat sides (as on a "pilgrim bottle") were originally designed for easy attachment to a pack animal but are here primarily a stylistic convention. The cast iron body is beautifully damascened in gold and silver with the eight Buddhist emblems encircling a *shou* emblem and paired dragons, with a fret pattern on the base. The dragon handle, *makura* spout, and lotus finial are of brass. *Cat. no. 94.*

COVERED TEA BOWL

The body of this bowl is constructed of finely grained ivory with coral, turquoise and silver wire mountings in the Nepalese style. The silver stepped dome lid and interior silver lining of the bowl appear to be Tibetan workmanship. The lid combines repoussé, openwork, and incising in a decoration of lotus scroll and Chinese auspicious emblems, with a coral finial. *Cat. no. 96.*

Monks blowing trumpets on a monastery
roof, Lhasa, 1937.

Ritual and Ceremony

The Tibetan people's active engagement with the spiritual world existed on several levels. The most constant and mundane involvement was the daily manipulation of objects to magically protect the individual and the community. Although incorporated into the Buddhist framework, basically this was an indigenous folk religion, an emotional response to a harsh environment, an attempt to cope with the natural and supernatural forces at work in the mountains, rivers, and sky.

Prayer flags, prayer wheels, rosaries, and charmboxes were owned and used by all Tibetans. Prayers, *mantras*, auspicious emblems, and powerful substances were contained in these prayer devices, serving to protect their owner as well as contribute to his spiritual advancement. These prayers helped to create a spiritual envelope around the individual and his possessions, deflecting destructive forces.

Priests provided these devices, sanctified them, and performed ceremonies when more powerful ritual involvement was necessary. In pre-Buddhist Tibet, a shaman figure performed these services and this sort of magically endowed person continued, under Buddhism, to function as village priest and doctor. Since the 15th century and the organization of a state religion, however, the monastery, with its hierarchy of monks and officials, dominated the spiritual life of all Tibetans.[1] Local monasteries ranging in size from small hermitages to immense universities contained thousands of monks, supervised the making and consecration of devices of spiritual power.

Monks from the monasteries officiated at home altars on the occasion of births, deaths, and illness, and advised on astrological matters. Family altars were of a size and splendor in keeping with the position of the owner but usually contained the vital elements for prayer and meditation: butter lamps for light, bowls for water and food offerings, and incense burners around some central sacred object or group of objects such as a book, image, or painting. Devices manipulated by monks for certain ceremonies were kept at the altar or brought in for the occasion: holy-water vases, musical instruments and ritual weapons.

Tibetan laymen could also erect (with the assistance of religious advisors) monuments to mark holy sites, mountain passes, entrances to important buildings, and to commemorate the deaths of family members. The erection of such a monument was a way for laymen to gain special spiritual merit. In the out-of-doors these monuments took the form of *chortens*, the Tibetan version of the Indian Buddhist reliquary mound, and piles of stones inscribed with prayers ("*mani* stones").

On the great festivals of the yearly cycle (the New Year, saints' days, harvests, etc.), ceremonies involving chanting, music, dancing, and presentation of special ritual objects were performed by the congregation of monks. These performances took place in monastery courtyards or in an open space large enough to accommodate assemblies. These occasions were an opportunity for laymen to witness and absorb a more intense level of spiritual activity. Giant paintings, appliques, and images could be viewed, circumambulated, and perhaps touched at this time. Scriptures were recited and "morality plays" presented. The power and magnificence of the Buddhist faith, and the hierarchy which explained and preserved that faith, were thus made manifest, renewing and reinforcing the daily devotions of the common man.

The church, housed in the imposing architecture of its monasteries, pursued its own activities between these ceremonial occasions. The primary goal of the monastic community was spiritual enlightenment and to this end it remained aloof from the rest of the population which supported the monastery's earthly needs.[2] This arrangement, so like the situation of the European peasant with the medieval Catholic Church, was mutually beneficial if one accepted the vital importance of ritual protection for the society.

From the 15th to 20th centuries the Buddhist establishment in Tibet and regions of Mongolia and China, was dominated by the Gelugpa sect. Gradually

The great *chorten* of Gyantse, built in the 15th century, 1935.

Gartok monastery showing its typically Tibetan assemblage of chapels, assembly halls, and apartments on a steep mountain slope, Mar Kham, 1917.

taking over the secular powers of the ancient Tibetan kings and the vassal princes, the Gelugpa ("Yellow Hat") sect overshadowed the older ("Red Hat" or unreformed) sects such as the Sakyapa, Kagyudpa, and Nyingmapa. Powerful Gelugpa religious leaders, such as Tsong-kha-pa (1357-1419), the 5th Dalai Lama (1617-1682)[3], and the 13th Dalai Lama (1876-1933) unified Tibet and effectively guided the political, economic, and spiritual concerns of the nation. During times when the Dalai Lama was weak or in his minority, however, opposing religious sects within Tibet, and Mongolians, Chinese, Nepalese, or British (in India) on her borders, harassed and disrupted Tibetan autonomy. From its first entry into the plateau in the 7th century, the Buddhist church aligned itself with temporal power and it enjoyed the privileges but also suffered the consequences of such power in the succeeding centuries.

Tibetan Buddhism surrounded itself with physical manifestations of its power and splendor. Monasteries were awe-inspiring structures suggesting, and often serving as fortresses. Monks of high rank dressed in rich robes and were treated like royalty. The fine silver objects from the Batang monastery, (see also p. 60 and Cat. nos. 122a & b, 127 a & b, 129, 130 a & b and 131 a & b), all of Derge workmanship, are proof of the glory of the church even in a provincial area. Abbots and learned *lamas* were regarded as living vessels of spiritual forces. This assumption of sacred qualities in a living person was epitomized by the idea of incarnate *lamas* such as the Dalai Lama and Panchen Lama.

A repertoire of movements and sounds was developed by the Tibetan clergy, quite distinct from the rituals of Buddhism in other Asian countries, to aid in the journey toward spiritual mastery. Magical implements such as the *dorje* and *phurpa* extended the power of the monks and were vital elements in the success of blessing and exorcising ceremonies. Music was also an important aspect of all Tibetan ritual. Chanting and singing invoked particular texts and *mantras*, and was accompanied by the music of drums, trumpets, and cymbals. The combined sounds of voices and instruments created an intense and hypnotic atmosphere. Hand gestures and body movements were used with music in elaborate ceremonies. Examinations for the attainment of theological degrees involved discussions of texts by teacher and student accompanied with forceful and symbolic body movements. Mysterious and graceful, these "dances" expressed the harmonious use of the physical and mental equipment of the body. This combination of sound and movement was amplified by the addition of masks and costumes in religious operas. Here the monks assumed the roles of gods and demons and enacted complex stories of the supernatural world. The operas provided a mystical interaction with the spiritual world, served as a meditational exercise for the performers, and as morality plays for the audience.

[1] A non-Buddhist religion and priesthood, called Bön, continued to exist in relative harmony with the Buddhist church into the 20th century. Bön is believed to be an organized form of the pre-Buddhist Tibetan faith.

[2] This independence was, however, tempered by the laymen's daily need for religious guidance. In addition, since families sent their sons (and infrequently, their daughters) into the monasteries and usually continued to support them during their student years and beyond, and since the monasteries (as part of the State) owned or controlled the land and economy of the area, there was a constant practical interaction between the ecclesiastic and lay communities.

[3] The title Dalai Lama ("Ocean of Wisdom") was conferred on the head of the Gelugpa sect, Sodnam Gyatsho, in 1578 by Altan Khan (Chief of the Tumed branch of the Mongol Empire). Sodnam Gyatsho referred to himself as the 3rd Dalai Lama, giving the title as well to his two predecessors.

Note: Names of deities in this section are given in their most common Sanskrit or Tibetan form. Tibetan (T.) transliterated names or terms are provided as well, when appropriate. The objects illustrated were made in Tibet in the 18th to 20th centuries unless otherwise noted.

Pile of *mani* stones around a central carved wood staff, near Batang, Kham, ca. 1920.

LARGE BUTTER LAMP

The incised Tibetan inscription on the base of this lamp reads, "In the water-dog year, on an auspicious day of the second Tibetan month, the world was illuminated by this precious vessel. Designed and cut by the three lamas: Kel-sang Wang-den, Lob-sang Don-t'rup and Lob-sang Gyen-tshen. Carved out of the second precious metal, containing 30 Chinese oz., 4 *sho* and 2 1/2 *kar*, it is a joyful offering."

The Tibetan 60-year cyclical calendar combines the five elements with the 12 zodiac animals. The last water-dog year before 1920 was 1862. A *sho* is 1/10 of a Chinese ounce, a *kar* is 1/10 of a *sho*. Symbolic of the sacred flame, and used to illuminate altars, such lamps were filled with yak, cow, or goat butter which fueled burning cotton wicks. *Cat. no. 123.*

PAIR OF MAKURA FINIALS

Such finials were set at the termination of eaves on monastery roofs. They functioned as guardian spirits to ward off evil. These finials are particularly vivid castings with attached curled tongues coming out of the gaping fanged mouths. *Cat. no. 137 a & b.*

RUG

The design of this rug, one of a pair, is formed of wool pile on a cotton warp and weft and shows a classic Chinese theme of dragon and pearl amidst clouds, sea and mountains. The Tibetan inscription across the top reads, "The offering of the Doctor of Divinity Ngag-dbang'od-zer" (the patron of rugs). The mate to this example has the design, including the inscription, as a mirror image. The rugs would have been wrapped around four-sided pillars in temple chanting halls so that the dragon bodies appeared to encircle the pillar. Obviously made for a specific Tibetan commission, the rugs were probably woven in Ninghsia, China, a center for such wool carpet production. *Cat. no. 138.*

CHARMBOX

Charms to ward away evil spirits were worn by all Tibetans around their necks or chest. Ornamental boxes such as this, in the shape of a shrine, were placed on household altars and strapped around the chest for traveling (when special protection against harm was necessary). The charms contained in these boxes might include written prayers, small images, and auspicious objects. In addition to the prayers, image, or amulets enclosed in the box, the decoration of lotus, *garuda*, bowl of offerings, and auspicious emblems gave ritual significance to the charmbox. *Cat. no. 114.*

MOLD FOR DOUGH EFFIGIES

This six-sided wood board is carved with incised images of animals, fantastic figures, and emblems. The use of dough effigies as scapegoats (T. *glud*) to propitiate malignant spirits or as offerings to protective deities seems to derive from pre-Buddhist Tibetan custom. Before Buddhism forbade such practices, Tibetan shamans made animal and human sacrifices to tribal gods. The dough effigies were thus a substitute in accommodation to Buddhist philosophy. *Cat. no. 117.*

MANI STONE

Pieces of shale with "*Om mani padme hum*" in low relief and polychrome paint on their face, were common Tibetan prayer offerings. This *mantra* "*Om*, the jewel in the lotus, *hum*" was the most frequently heard and written Buddhist prayer in Tibet. Invoking Avalokitesvara, patron deity of Tibet, the six syllables were believed to aid the freeing of sentient beings from the bonds of earthly existence and to give merit to those chanting the prayer. Special virtue was accrued to those who carved (or paid an artisan to carve) *mani* prayers on stones to be left in piles or walls marking holy sites (see p. 59). *Cat. no. 119.*

WHEEL OF THE LAW

The wheel is a complex symbol in Buddhist Asia, recalling the sun with its halo of flames, the setting of the law of Buddhism in motion, and, in Tibet, Burma, and Thailand, serving as an emblem of sovereignty. This particular wheel is believed to have been the symbol of office of the 6th Panchen Lama (died 1780), smuggled to Kham during the Nepalese invasions of Southern Tibet (including Shigatse and the seat of the Panchen Lama, Tashilhunpo) in 1791-2. It was in the possession of the Jö Lama in Batang. The quality of the silver and workmanship is similar to the butter lamps from the Crane/Shelton collections, known to have been made in Derge, Kham. The silver repoussé which form the two identical sides of the wheel and the base are pegged together around a central core, the composition of which is unknown. If the wheel is ever opened, its contents may confirm the connection to the Panchen Lama. *Cat. no. 134.*

BANNER

Such banners were used to decorate the sides of large monastery altars. This pair was appliqued in Central Tibet from imported silks dating from the 18th to the 19th centuries. The "monster mask" plaque with flaming jewel sides and finial provides ritual protection; the long (over 19 feet) streamers of fine Chinese brocade have a design of dragons, sea, and sky, symbolic of the celestial and worldly realms. *Cat. no. 136a.*

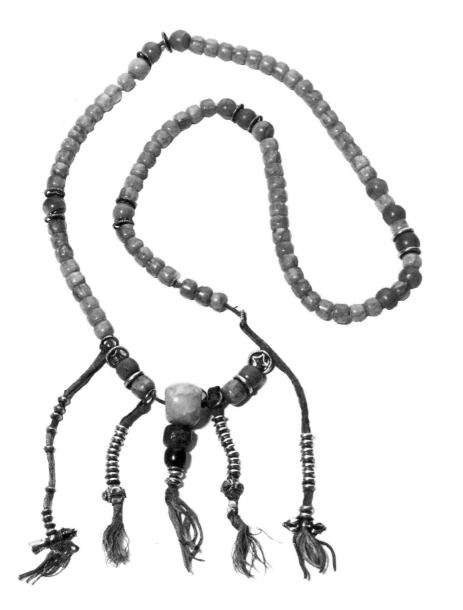

DANCE COSTUME

This sort of elaborate costume was worn by monk dancers for the religious operas presented on ceremonial occasions during the year. The loose style of the robe may derive from Central Asian shamanist or Chinese theatrical tradition. The mask represents one of the fierce guardian kings incorporated into Tibetan Buddhism from local tribal gods. *Cat. nos. 144-146.*

ROSARY

Buddhist rosaries, evolved from the ancient Hindu prayer beads, were used by both laymen and monks in China, Japan, and Tibet. In Tibet, rosaries were supposed to consist of 108 beads, a number sacred to Buddhists. The main beads were used to count repetitions of prayers, the counters (attached at the bottom) recorded multiples of the main beads, thus counting thousands of repetitions. *Cat. no. 112.*

PRAYER WHEEL

Owned and used by Tibetans of every social rank, prayer wheels were devices for

creating prayers by hand power. Rolls of written prayers or *mantras* were sealed in the cylinder; with each revolution, the prayers were "sent out." Cylinders containing prayers were also set up on roofs or in streams, with blades to turn them by wind or water power. Giant wheels were placed outside temples to be turned by passing pilgrims and monks. *Cat. no. 111.*

SADDLE CLOTH AND COVER

This saddle set was probably used on a living mule, to accompany an oracle-priest personifying Lhamo, the fierce protector goddess who uses her son's flayed skin, shown here as a double skin with legs bound together, for a saddle cloth. The applique work is unusually fine, with the flayed skin padded to stand out from the polychrome wave ("sea of blood") background, on the cloth, and a carefully designed crossed *dorje* and *yin-yang* center on the cover. The shape of both cloth and cover are typical of Chinese style saddle paraphernalia used by laymen (see p. 22). *Cat. no. 150a & b.*

DANCER'S APRON

This apron was worn as part of the costume of a monk personifying Yama, lord of death, in one of the religious operas. The robe and mask of such a costume would have been similar to those on p. 67. *Cat. no. 149.*

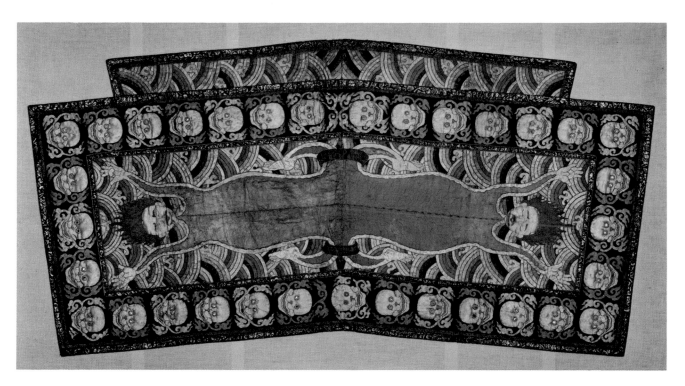

MASK

Wood masks were used less frequently than those of papier mâché (see p. 67) due to the scarcity of this material in Tibet. This example portrays a fierce guardian king. It would be worn with a costume by monk dancers for the religious operas. *Cat. no. 147.*

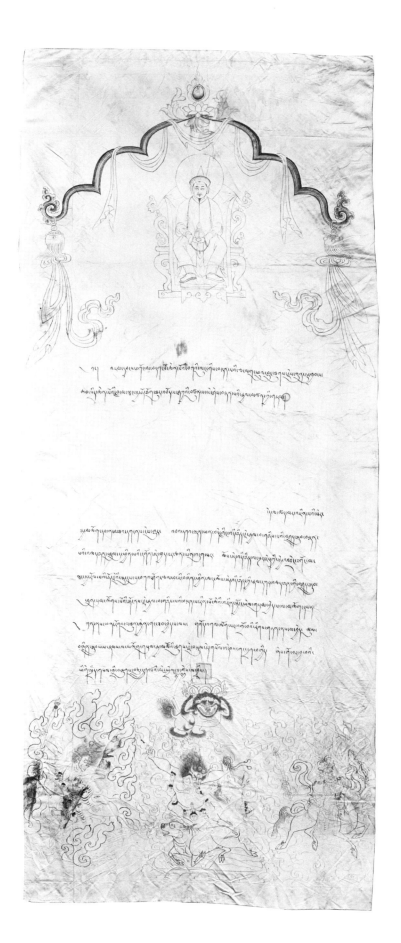

DECREE OF THE PEKING LAMA

The painting above the inscription shows the figure of Lcang-skya Lalita Vajra, Grand Lama of Peking, on a throne holding a vase of holy water; below are the figures of Lhamo on her mule, Yama and Yami treading on a bull and prostrate figure, and a guardian king on horseback. The Tibetan inscription is addressed to the residents of Gah-dan Penda-ling Monastery, Batang, endorsing and honoring the Batang Lama, and bestowing absolution and grace. The document is dated in accordance with 1776 (during the reign of the Chinese Emperor, Ch'ien Lung) and signed with Lcang-skya's personal seal, above, and official (square) seal supported by a lion, below. *Cat. no. 151.*

MINIATURE CHORTEN

This miniature *chorten* retains the simple Indian form of medieval reliquary mounds (*stupas*). Symbolic of divine wisdom, it was an essential element on monastery or home altars. Like the large stone and wood *chortens* found throughout the Tibetan countryside (see p. 56), these miniatures in metal contained relics or precious substances and often commemorated important individuals. The original Indian Buddhist *stupa* symbolized the Buddha's *Parinirvana* (death and permanent attainment of *nirvana*). This meaning was retained in the Tibetan *chorten* with an added parasol symbolic of universal spiritual emperor-ship. *Cat. no. 135.*

LIBATION EWER

This graceful ewer is in the form of a Chinese wine receptacle of the Ming period (1368-1644) and may be of Chinese workmanship. The design features typical Chinese elements, incised cranes and clouds (on lid), pomegranates, festoons, horses, waves, and mountains, and a relief medallion of paired dragons (on body), with the common Tibetan *makura* spout and dragon handle. *Cat. no. 159.*

DORJE AND BELL

The *dorje* ("diamond scepter") and bell were used together by monks, held in the right and left hands, respectively, to convey the mystical union of compassion with wisdom. The *dorje* has four prongs springing from *makura* heads around a center post at each end, with lotus petals decorating the central caps. The handle of the bell is similar to the *dorje* but has eight prongs, attached to a central post over the head of Prajna, symbol of supreme wisdom. The bell section is decorated with Sanskrit syllables, lotus petals, *dorjes* and "monster masks." An iron clapper, suspended from the apex of the interior, produces a clear, brilliant tone as the bell is manipulated. *Cat. nos. 154 a & b.*

PHUR-PA

An important "weapon" in exorcist ceremonies, the *phur-pa* stabs demons of the air. Examples in bronze or iron are more common than the painted wood type shown here but all share the triangular blade form. The handle here has a complex assemblage of endless knots between the heads of a ferocious deity (a manifestation of Padma Sambhava? see p. 103) and of a *makura*, from whose mouth the entwined snakes and blade issues. Since such implements are not found in the magical weapon repertoire of Indian mythology, it is speculated that the *phurpa* is a native Tibetan or Central Asian form. *Cat. no. 157.*

BOWL AND STAND

Thin translucent jade or porcelain bowls and cups imported from China were the preferred food and beverage vessels for clergy and nobles. Paired here with a repouseé silver stand of lotus design, the jade bowl may have contained rice or other food for ceremonial use at an altar or have been used for actual consumption at a ritual meal. *Cat. no. 161 a & b.*

CHOPPER

The chopper was a magical weapon used against demonic forces in ceremonies. Its handle resembles the *dorje* on p. 72, cast in one solid piece and attached to the separate curved blade which issues from a fierce *makura* head. Such a "weapon" would only be used by a specially trained priest. *Cat. no. 156.*

TEAPOT

Based on the form of the common copper, brass, or wood Tibetan teapot (see p. 37), this magnificent silver piece was intended for ceremonial use by high-ranking members of the clergy, as was the bowl and stand, p. 75. The dragon on the handle and *makura* on the spout symbolize the life-giving power of water, especially appropriate to tea, a basic food of the Tibetans, and the lotus finial symbolizes purity. *Cat. no. 160.*

CRESTED HAT, MITRE SHAPED HAT, AND ABBOT'S HAT

Hats were not part of the original Indian Buddhist monks' attire but figured prominently in the official and ceremonial equipment of Tibetan monks. The mitre shaped and crested hats recall a long tradition of peaked cloth headgear in Central Asia; perhaps Tibet borrowed from this military/official tradition to develop its own unique system of ecclesiastical headgear. Statuettes from the Oxus Treasure (Turkestan, 5th century B.C.) and tribute bearers on reliefs at Persepolis (Iran, 6th-5th century B.C.) wear variations of peaked hats and hoods. A stiff-brimmed hat is seen on guardian deities of Mongolian origin and was one of the types of hats worn to commemorate the ancient kings of Tibet in the New Year festival. The gold lacquered hat shown here was worn by high officials of the Gelugpa sect. The red mitre shaped hat is the type worn by pre-reformation sects such as the Nyingmapa and Sakyapa. The sun-moon emblem is associated with Padma-Sambhava (see p. 103). The yellow hat at left is a slightly higher-crested version of the hat worn by all Gelugpa monks (see p. 55). *Cat. nos. 141-143.*

MUSICAL INSTRUMENTS

Ritual music in Tibet was a powerful element in all ceremonies and an important aid to spiritual pursuits. The instruments which created the music, providing background and punctuation to the basic sounds of chanting, were completely different from those for secular use. Though restricted to drums, trumpets, and cymbals, the temple orchestras achieved complex rhythms and tones through the varied sizes and shapes. Drums ranged from large double-headed wood and leather instruments beaten with a stick (p. 79) to small rattle drums shaken rapidly so that attached clappers hit each of the double heads (p. 81). Trumpets, always in pairs, were especially numerous and varied from the immense telescopic examples seen in the photograph on pp. 54-55 to the shorter types seen on p. 80. In all Tibetan trumpets, the sound is manipulated solely by the player's lips vibrating against the mouth piece and the force of the blowing; there are no finger holes. Large cymbals were struck together on their edges or clanged together with great force to create delicate or clamorous sounds, depending on the music (p. 81).

As in all Tibetan ritual objects, the physical structure of the temple instruments was crucial to their ritual power. The rich use of brass, copper, silver, and wood was augmented by precious stones and symbolic decoration or by forms of special significance, such as the dragon heads (p. 80). Substances such as skulls, bones, horns, and shells were also incorporated into instruments of particular ceremonial use.

These forms, in company with the psychological state of the players and singers in the orchestras, produced a profound and unique sound which has no parallels in other Asian music, creating a mystical experience transcending the rhythm and noises of the "real" world.

SERPENTINE TRUMPET
Cat. no. 172.

PAIR OF TRUMPETS
Cat. nos. 173a & b.

LARGE DRUM WITH BEATER
Cat. nos. 163a & b.

WELK HORN

Conch or welk horns have an ancient association in India with the god Vishnu. They are used in Hindu and Buddhist ceremonies as offering vessels and as trumpets. In Tibet, shell trumpets were used in temple orchestras and, alone, to summon monks to service and to invoke water and rain. *Cat. no. 170.*

PAIR OF DRAGON TRUMPETS

Cat. no. 171a & b.

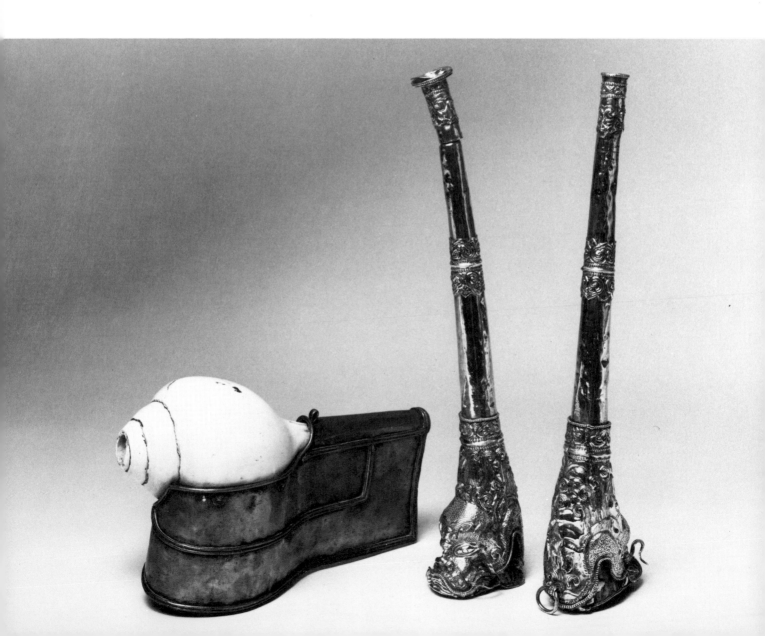

SKULL DRUM AND SMALL RATTLE DRUM

Cat. nos. 164 & 165.

PAIR OF LARGE CYMBALS

Held vertically, this type of cymbal beats the rhythm of the temple orchestra in company with rattle drums. Cymbals have a long history of use in India and are seen held by celestial musicians in Buddhist and Hindu schemes of heaven. *Cat. no. 175a & b.*

SMALL CYMBALS

The discs are held suspended from the chain and their edges struck, emitting a high piercing tone which continues (diminishing in strength) as long as the discs are allowed to vibrate. Such cymbals were used in funeral ceremonies and in calling the "hungry spirits." *Cat. no. 176.*

Monks working on a colored grain *mandala*, Drepung monastery, Lhasa, 1937.

The artist Tsering completing a *tanka*,
Norbu Linga, Lhasa, 1937.

The Spiritual World

Tibetan sculpture, painting, and appliques were, like the ritual and ceremonial pieces discussed in the preceding section, made by or under the supervision of Buddhist priests and had a liturgical function. Once made and consecrated,[1] these objects were empowered with the mystic energy of the divinities which they represented. In meditating upon or praying to such a visualization, the individual sought to absorb its spiritual essence. To someone outside the Tibetan Buddhist culture, this liturgical function can be only indirectly appreciated but the psychological intensity of this art is communicated across cultural barriers.

Tibetan images and paintings in Western collections are primarily of portable size and lasting material, showing but a few forms of a wonderfully varied artistic tradition. Gigantic "paintings" were made and stored in the large monasteries to be unrolled, usually once a year for specific occasions, on building walls (see p. 8) or down bare mountainsides (see p. 86). These magnificent and awe-inspiring creations were constructed of appliqued or embroidered cloths able to withstand the rigors of the once-a-year viewing. Appliqued and embroidered horizontal banners in a medium scale were displayed in the large chanting halls for particular services. The banner on p. 117 has probably been removed from such a horizontal appliqued series. Tankas in this medium were in the same format as their painted counterparts and are well represented in Western collections.

Over-life-size images, made of clay, wood, or metal were the common focal point of large monastery altars; few of these have left Tibet. Large images, made of butter, were another important type of sculpture, executed for specific ceremonies and then burned or dispersed. Temporary "paintings" of colored grain were also constructed for rituals and destroyed at their conclusion. The interior surfaces of Tibetan monasteries were covered with wall paintings which provided a rich visual context for the three-dimensional images.

Fortunately, the paintings and images preserved in Western collections present the full range of iconographic and stylistic types in the Tibetan repertoire. The portable small scale banners (tankas) and miniature paintings in books show the polychrome brilliance and energy of the best Tibetan painting. Except for some rare silk examples, tankas were constructed of cotton cloth sized with lime water and animal glue, then polished with a piece of shell to form a smooth non-porous surface. The colors were ground mineral and vegetable substances mixed with lime water and gluten. Constrained by iconographic rules of placement and form, the tanka artist expressed his genius in the glowing juxtaposition of jewel-like color.

Giant embroidered banner displayed once
a year at Labrang, Amdo, ca. 1930.

Small scale metal images ably convey the Tibetan sculptor's sensitive use of the tactile and tonal possibilities of this medium. Wood was infrequently used due to its scarcity. The small number of wood images known in Western collections lack the finesse of the abundant Nepalese examples. The same is true of stone sculpture, often encountered in Himalayan art but rare in Tibet. Relief carving of prayers and images was popular on the living rock, but Tibetan sculptors seemed uninterested in working three-dimensionally in stone. In metal, however, these artists were quite obviously at ease. Greatly influenced by the refined bronze casting, in the lost wax process, of Northeastern India and Kashmir as early as the 7th to the 10th centuries, Tibetan sculptors later adopted the techniques of Nepalese repoussé and cast gilt copper modeling. From the 16th to 20th centuries, the Chinese style of gilt bronze sculpture was added to the Tibetan repertoire.

In these instances of cross-cultural borrowing, both artisans and art objects were brought into Tibet where private and church patrons eagerly sought the finest workmanship. Foreign influence is apparent as well in painting, where the traditions of India (transmitted through Nepal and Kashmir), Central Asia and China can all be seen. The technique of applique can be traced to ancient Central Asian felt and leather garments and animal trappings. The Tibetan use of applique for creating religious pictures probably was inspired by Chinese woven and embroidered icons.

Despite all this borrowed inheritance, there is a unifying and uniquely Tibetan quality of self-possession which pervades these visualizations. The paintings and images seem to have their own controlling forces and emotional moods, ranging from the centered calm of the Paradise of Amitayus (p. 110) to the demonic frenzy of the Dharmapala (p. 97). Mystical and visionary, the liturgical art of Tibet portrays a reality beyond the world of everyday perceptions.

---

[1] Metal images were hollowcast or repoussé; wood images had excavated interiors. Both types were filled with charms, written prayers, and auspicious objects, their bases sealed when consecrated. Two-dimensional painted, appliqued, and embroidered hangings often had dedicatory inscriptions and marks on the back.

Note: All objects illustrated in this section were made in Tibet unless otherwise noted. Names of deities are given in their most common Sanskrit or Tibetan form. Tibetan (T.) transliterated names are provided when appropriate.

TARA

This image of the savioress, the female counterpart of Avalokitesvara, was made in Nepal (or by Nepalese craftsmen working in Tibet) perhaps in the 17th century. Since Shelton obtained it in Kham, the image is evidence for the movement of religious objects (and craftsmen) even across the great distance between Nepal and Eastern Tibet. The goddess is shown in a pose similar to the earlier *devi* (see p. 94). The "string" drapery is one of the Nepalese conventions for the diaphanous garments of the gods. One earring is a large tube, found on early images and signifying the male element in Tara's personality. Her empty left hand once held a lotus. The base and *mandorla* may have originally been from other images; the base is strangely bent and rather wide for this figure while the *mandorla* is too small. *Cat. no. 188a & b.*

VAJRADHARA

Vajradhara, "Bearer of the Thunderbolt," is a manifestation of the Adi-Buddha (see also p. 98); he holds the *dorje* and bell crossed at his chest in the gesture of "highest energy." The graceful, attenuated body, rich ornamentation and fine gilding show a blend of Nepalese and Chinese influence. 17th century. *Cat. no. 178.*

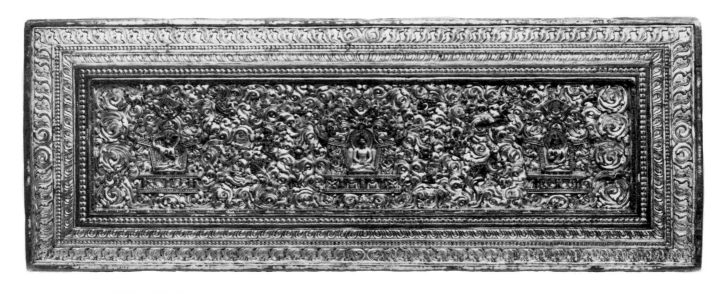

BOOK COVER

The exquisite carving on the top of this cover depicts a Buddha in meditation at center with Majusri, Bodhisattva of Wisdom, at left and another Bodhisattva at right, each seated in complex aureole/thrones with *garuda* and *makuras* (at center), "monster masks" and geese, lion and elephants (at both sides). Undulating vine scrolls "grow" out from under the central Buddha and fill the entire central field, populated here and there by delightful fantastic lions, peacocks, horses, monkeys, and geese. A lotus blossom and a lotus bud are at the left and right of the center throne. Encircling the middle recessed area are bands of beading, lotus petals, and vine scrolls, organized so as to move gracefully from the center of the long and short sides outward to the corners. The traces of paint and over-all gilding appear to be applied over damaged areas in the wood carving; it must therefore be a later, though extremely fine, regilding and painting of the original surface. The underside of the cover has a flat painted geometric pattern of rows of circles formed of thin concentric lines on a red background. One end side of the cover is carved with a vine scroll, at the center of which is the Tibetan letter *Kha*, signifying the second volume. The text and bottom cover of this book are now lost (see p. 91 for a complete assemblage of a manuscript).

Tibetan books copied Indian tradition as transmitted through either Nepal or Kashmir. This cover is an interesting amalgum of Nepali heritage in the geometric painting of the underside and the delicately carved gods and animals on the top, along with a Kashmiri size and format. Books of this type were first assembled in the 14th century in Tibet; the original carving of this cover is perhaps of 16th century date. *Cat. no. 181.*

FOLIO FROM A VOLUME OF THE KANJUR (detail)

The folio is a title page from a volume of the *Satasahasrika Prajna-paramita* (T. *bKa'-gyur Sher-phyin 'bum*), "Transcendental Wisdom in 100,000 slokas," discourses addressed by Shakyamuni Buddha to celestial beings, written ca. first century B.C. A cloth tab, probably later in date than the page, gives, in black ink, the letter of the Tibetan alphabet (which indicates the volume number) and a brief title. The folio is from a set of 14 books in the Museum's collection, obtained by Shelton in Batang. The illuminated title pages, and in some volumes additional illustrated pages, are in several styles, suggesting that the earlier pages such as shown here were added to and replaced by later folios as the manuscripts were used in the monastery. The earlier pages are in the style of Western Tibet indicating that these were either made in the West and carried at some point to Batang in Eastern Tibet or that Western Tibetan artists were brought to Batang to illuminate the volumes. These two folios may be 16th to 17th century in date. *Cat. no. 182a.*

A VOLUME OF THE KANJUR

This volume is an abbreviated form of the main *Sutras* of the *Kanjur* (*bKa'-gyur*) often used as a single book. It was made in Lhasa as part of the dowry of the bride of a prince of Batang. She carried it to Eastern Tibet for her marriage in 1890. The top page is set with pearls and turquoises and has the salutation, "In the language of India, 'Holy Teaching of Transcendental Wisdom in 8,000 slokas.' In the language of Tibet, 'Holy Teaching of Transcendental Wisdom in 8,000 slokas, Chapter one'" between two "all-powerful ten" symbols. *Cat. no. 183 a-c.*

AVALOKITESVARA

The four-armed form of Avalokitesvara, Bodhisattva of Mercy, is believed to incarnate in the Dalai Lama. He is seated in meditation holding a rosary and lotus and offering a devotional gesture. Attendant Bodhisattvas echo his hand gestures. Surrounding them is a charming paradise scene. The lotus pedestal arises from a pond in which ducks and jewels float. The spiritual "father" of Avalokitesvara, Amitabha, sits above the halo of light and gorgeous lotus blossoms. This applique is still in its original setting of fine Chinese and (on the back) Indian silks. The frame and "curtain" are standard finishing details, sewn on to all appliqued, embroidered, and painted *tankas* of the 18th to 20th centuries. The inner border of red and yellow silk symbolizes the radiant power and wisdom of the deities depicted, the blue outer border symbolizes the universe of sky and earth, the rectangular patch represents the cosmic waters. 18th century. *Cat. no. 186.*

CROWNED BUDDHA

Dressed in the traditional monk's robes of the historic Buddha, this image has a crown and earrings to signify its position as a celestial sovereign. The hands form the gesture of "turning the wheel of the law." The heavy casting and refined workmanship are typically Chinese. During the Yuan and Ming periods, the Mongol and Chinese Emperors had Tibetan lamas as religious advisors and the Tibetan Buddhist Church was particularly favored. This image dates from the Ming period (1368-1644). *Cat. no. 179.*

DEVI ("goddess")

This small exquisite goddess, embodying the fecundity and energy of the female element, is an example of 11th century Nepalese workmanship. She holds a fruit or boss in her right hand and lotus in her left. It is difficult to determine whether she represents the Buddhist goddess Tara or one of the Hindu *devis*, as both were worshipped in this form in Nepal. Such images, the Napalese distillation of the more robust Indian originals, were carried into Tibet as early as the 9th century and strongly influenced the development of indigenous Tibetan sculpture. In addition, Nepalese metal artisans for centuries worked on commissions for Tibetan monasteries and private patrons and thus had a continuing impact on Tibetan three-dimensional art into the 20th century.
Cat. no. 187.

MANDALA OF VASUDHARA

A *mandala* is the sphere of power surrounding a deity, often expressed in Tibetan painting as an idealized "world" of
geometric configurations. Vasudhara,
Goddess of Abundance, is shown here at
the center of the *mandala* and in eight
identical emanations in the surrounding
lotus petals. Each holds a jewel and stalk
of grain and has offerings at her feet. On
the heart of each goddess a *mantra* of Tibetan letters revolves around her *bija*
(root) *mantra*. Each *mantra* is different.
The outer ring of writing includes the
donor's call for blessing on the work with
three repetitions of the Sanskrit alphabet
(in Tibetan). The painting may have been
intended as a charm, to be folded and carried or placed in an image. 18th to 19th
centuries. *Cat. no. 190.*

DHARMAPALA

This energetic figure is a six-armed "Defender of the Faith" draped in swirling scarves, snakes, skulls, and flayed skins. In addition to the trident and noose, he carries a dagger, skull-cup and one missing weapon, and gestures menacingly with his primary left hand. A half-*dorje* sits amidst his flaming hair. The specific identity of this *Dharmapala* has not been determined; one unusual feature is the bird-headed creature (*garuda?*) being trampled underfoot. The frenzied quality of this sculpture is enhanced by the crude workmanship, visible also on another early piece, p. 101; in both of these, the artist's swift manipulation of the lost wax process is still apparent in the metal casting. The guardian's close relationship to early Chinese forms of *Dharmapalas* indicates a date in the 12th to 13th centuries. *Cat. no. 192.*

MANDALA OF THE FIERCE AND TRANQUIL DEITIES

This rare painting portrays a phase of the teachings of the *Bar-do Thos-grol* ("Tibetan Book of the Dead") in which deities appear to the deceased, products of his confused desire for existence, in his passage to the region of rebirth. The painting is organized into a schematic *mandala* form with all the secondary deities radiating around the central figure, three-headed winged Chichok Heruka. This "knowledge-holding" deity appears in embrace with his female partner, his six arms hold a trident, mirror, *dorje*, bell, noose, and skull-cup, and his six legs tread on human figures. Similar flaming Heruka Buddhas and consorts surround the center. The ferocious energy of the assembly of animal and human form protectors is interwoven with the calm beneficence of the Buddhas and Bodhisattvas arrayed over a mountain and sky landscape. Each group of deities is identified with Tibetan captions. The teachings illustrated here are especially important to the esoteric Nyingmapa tradition. 17th to 18th centuries. *Cat. no. 191.*

VAJRASATTVA

Vajrasattva, "Whose Essence is the Thunderbolt," as a manifestation of the Adi ("First") Buddha, shown as a Bodhisattva and representative of the celestial origin of all phenomena. The wide and schematic face of this image is unusual but the olive tone bronze, use of inlay, and powerfully modeled body indicate that it was cast in Western Tibet under the vestigial influence of Kashmir in the 15th to the 16th centuries. *Cat. no. 177.*

VAJRAPANI

The "Wielder of the Thunderbolt" steps on four serpents and carries a fifth coiled in his left hand. More serpents adorn his neck, wrists, torso, and ankles. Jewels, skulls, and garlands encircle his flaming hair and a tiger skin is wrapped around his hips. The *dorje* symbol is foremost in Vajrapani's personality as he is the power force emanating from Aksobhya Buddha. The casting here is much more refined than in the one on p. 97, showing the influence of Nepalese metalwork. 17th to 18th centuries. *Cat. no. 193.*

BSE'I KHRAB CAN

("He who has a cuirass of leather"). Linear paintings are one form of Tibetan *tanka*; the choice of violent orange and the surprising use of limited modeling here give vivid expression to this angry deity. The laced armor from which bSe'i Khrab Can derives his name is one of the types of defensive attire known in China from the T'ang period (618-906 A.D.).

This celestial warrior is armed with a jewcled club, yak hair snare, bow and arrows, and sword. To further emphasize his exuberant appearance, banners sprout from his helmet, a standard rests at his arm and roaring flames envelop his body and that of his horse. The demonic face is related to those on p. 97 and p. 99 but here is quite wild and non-human. bSe'i Khrab Can is one of the purely Tibetan protective

gods, unconnected to an Indian prototype and thus may be one of the pre-Buddhist spirits of Tibet, "tamed" to the service of the imported religion. Six emanations surround the central deity, five on horses and one on a cock, gyrating *dakinis*, animals, and humans are at each side, the figures of three saints rest calmly on lotus thrones above. 19th century. *Cat. no. 194.*

DORJE PHUR-PA

Although lacking a female partner, this powerful image conforms in all respects to the iconography of the "indestructible stake," the deity manifest in all *phur-pa* "weapons" (see p. 74). Five of his hands hold a 9-pronged and a 5-pronged *dorje*, a tri-lobed leaf motif, a (broken) trident, and a *phur-pa*. A sixth hand gestures with an open palm. Above the three heads—one smiling, two grimacing—the hair is piled high and tied with a snake. Snakes also adorn his ears, neck, shoulders, wrists, and ankles of his four legs. Elephant and human skins are tied around his chest, and a tiger skin around his hips. This crudely cast image, rough and patched on the back, seems to be relatively free of foreign influence. The brassy quality of the metal and the distorted attempts to portray musculature, however, do show a relation to Kashmiri sculpture. 13th century (?). *Cat. no. 198.*

VAJRAVARAHI

The "Adamtine Sow," identified by the pig's head above her right ear, is the consort of Samvara and the highest form of *dakini* goddess (T. *mKah-hgro*, "walking in the sky"). Her ferocious face is adorned with a skull crown and wheel of the law earrings. A third wheel is on her ornate necklace. Her dancing form is supported entirely by the left leg which fits into a base (here a modern replacement). Silver images of this size are comparatively rare in Western collections. 17th to 18th centuries. *Cat. no. 199.*

PADMA SAMBHAVA

Following the precedent set for Sakyamuni Buddha, the founder of the religion, great historical figures in the history of Buddhism in Tibet have been sanctified and portrayed as icons. Padma Sambhava, "The Lotus Born" (in Tibetan, "Precious Teacher"), is the earliest of these transmitters of the faith. Padma Sambhava came from the Buddhist monastery of Nalanda in Bengal at the invitation of King Ti-song De-tsan in 747, and was responsible for the first great flowering of Buddhism in Tibet. The Nyingmapa sect especially reveres this saint as he founded their order and also built the first monastery, Sam-ye (see p. 118). Padma Sambhava holds a 5-pronged *dorje* in an open-palm gesture and a skull-cup. His magic wand of trident and skulls over a double *dorje* vase rests against his shoulder. The richly detailed robes (decorated with Sanskrit letters in back) are those of his Udayana birthplace in Central Asia. His characteristic mitre hat has a vulture's feather; he also wears large rings and floral ornaments at his ears. His blue hair hangs in heavy coils on both shoulders. Western Tibet, 15th to 16th centuries. *Cat. no. 200.*

PARADISE OF PADMA SAMBHAVA

This lyrical painting depicts the great teacher in his celestial palace atop the "copper-colored" mountain. He is attended by an assembly of disciples, saints, and deities; *dakinis*, musicians and protectors fill the aureole of the palace and the sky with Shakyamuni at the apex. Amitabha and Avalokitesvara, of whom Padma Sambhava was an earthly manifestation, reside in the upper levels of the palace. The guardians of the four quarters stand at the lower entrances. Temples, *chortens*, beautiful gardens, and ascetics' caves are placed around the mountain which rises out of a magic sea. In the lower lands, humans bring offerings to grotesque demons and violent acts are performed. The pastel color scheme and delicate drawing make this *tanka* an especially effective depiction of the bliss of paradise. 17th century. *Cat. no. 201.*

A BODHISATTVA

The suave sensuality of this young god is a late development of the mixed Sino-Nepalese style of sculpture noted on p. 89. The casting appears to be Chinese work but the ornate jewelry and drapery and delicate attitude of the figure come out of Nepalese tradition. Pegs attached to the feet (set now in a modern wood stand) would have been pinned to a metal base. This was probably one of two attendant Bodhisattvas flanking a larger central image of a Buddha as on p. 92. Bodhisattvas, "Essence of Enlightenment," are important deities functioning at a level more accessible to the human realm than the celestial Buddhas. Since this figure has been separated from his original context, it is impossible to determine which Bodhisattva he represents. 17th to 18th centuries. *Cat. no. 185.*

MILAREPA

Ths small yet exquisitely cast image represents a much beloved patriarch of the Tibetan faith, Milarepa ("cotton-clad Mila") who lived ca. 1038-1122 and was one of the founders of the Kagyudpa sect. Both his biography and his "100,000 Songs" were written down by his disciples (see p. 109) and survive today. He is shown here in rather elegant robes, the skirt gathered in pleats at the waist with a shawl draped over his left shoulder and lower body. His meditation band crosses his bare right shoulder and chest. Coiled rings are set in his long ear lobes and his hair falls in thick curls down his back. The more usual simple cotton robes of Milarepa are seen on p. 107. His right hand gestures at his ear in the manner characteristic to Milarepa (in the position used by South Asian singers for high notes); his left hand holds a skull-cup of jewels. He sits on an antelope skin over a lotus pedestal. A lotus bud grows up to support his right foot. The mellow quality of the metal and the use of inlay are typical of Western Tibet. 15th century or earlier. *Cat. no. 204.*

PAIR OF PORTRAIT IMAGES

At left is a portrait of Milarepa in the familiar pose (see p. 106) with right hand at his ear, dressed in a white garment with blue dots, his face and body painted gold, hair blue, with facial features in natural colors (eyes blue); at right is a portrait of an unidentified monk, shown in the classic pose of "earth touching" used for Shakyamuni Buddha, wearing red robes of traditional Tibetan style, his face and body painted gold, hair black, with facial features in natural colors (eyes blue). These two rare wood images are obviously part of a set of perhaps dozens of portraits of the patriarchs of the Kagyudpa sect. Very few wooden pieces, especially of this size, have survived. The images show extensive splitting and repairs under the paint surface; the last reapplication of paint (now badly flaking) was probably done in the 20th century at the monastery where they were housed. The rough yet powerful carving and painting are in a 15th century style but these portraits may have been made as recently as the 19th century. *Cat. no. 206 a & b.*

LAMA GYAWA RGOD-TSHANG-PA MGON-PO RDORJE

Lama "Victorious" rGod-tsang-pa (1189-1258) was a disciple of the founder of the 'Brug-pa school of the Kagyudpa sect. He lived in Western Tibet. The style of the bronze is consistent with that region and was perhaps made at the Drupthe monastery mentioned in the inscription on the base, in the 16th century. The fat body and round face of the monk have the appearance of true portraiture, although the piece was cast 300 years or more after the death of this saint. As in the wood images, p. 107, this portrait conveys great psychological power through the facial expression despite the rather stolid and conventionalized treatment of the body. *Cat. no. 208.*

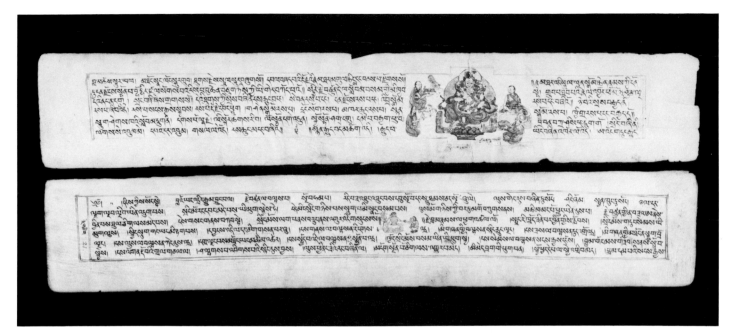

TWO FOLIOS FROM THE
BIOGRAPHY OF MILAREPA

Ascribed to the 12 disciples of Milarepa, the manuscript volume from which these folios are taken (244 folios in all), is perhaps a 17th to 18th century copy of an earlier work. Charming folk-like paintings are interspersed throughout the text. On the pages shown here, above, the text refers to the disciples of Milarepa and their illustrous descendants. The painting shows Jambhala, god of wealth, holding a peach (?) and mongoose. A bowl of offerings is placed before him, a monk sits with a manuscript on his lap at right, another offers jewels at left, and a woman, child and man, perhaps the book's patrons, present offerings at lower left and right. Below, Milarepa is shown in meditation with his sister Peta. The text discusses a famous scene in which the saint sings to Peta of the glorious merit in his ascetic life, to calm her fear at seeing his emaciated condition (in contrast to the elegant depiction of Milarepa on p. 106). *Cat. no. 205 a & b.*

PARADISE OF AMITAYUS

This superb *tanka,* though badly worn at the center and top, shows the glorious quality of Western Tibetan painting in the late 16th to early 17th centuries. This school of painting is usually called Gu-ge since it was in that area of Western Tibet that monastery wall paintings in this style were found in the mid-20th century. Gu-ge style paintings, a blend of early Nepali and Kashmiri traditions, are also known on monastery interiors in Ladakh (now part of India) and several Western Himalayan valleys. Buddhism flourished in these areas between the late 10th and the mid-17th centuries. Because of the destructive Muslim invasions of the Middle Ages and the general decline in power and wealth from the 17th to 20th centuries in this region, Gu-ge painting either in wall or *tanka* form is quite rare.

The strict ordering of the figures in this painting are typical of this style; the main deity, Amitayus (T. *Tshe-dpag-med*), "Buddha of Infinite Life," sits in meditation at the center on a lotus petal base holding the vase of the elixir of life. Gorgeous and fantastic flowers growing out of the vase are repeated behind all the deities in the painting. Amitayus wears robes with beautiful floral designs and jewelry set with precious gems. This form of attire is called *Sambhogakaya,* "body of light and bliss." Two standing Bodhisattvas flank the central image. The paradise setting, featuring lovely trees, pond, and birds recurs in all Tibetan depictions of the heavenly abodes (see p. 119), but it is here especially lyrical and beguiling. The artist has cleverly transformed the lower background of royal blue waters into the cloud-filled sky of the upper background with no discernable horizon. Repeated with slight variations at the left and right of the painting are Maitreya, the Buddha of the future in a mountain setting (top), Shakyamuni Buddha with Bodhisattva, saint, and human attendants (upper and lower center), and a group of six Bodhisattvas (center, left) and six saints (center, right). Perhaps the most delightful section of the painting is the lower area surrounding the stem which supports Amitayus' pedestal. Vines enclose two peacocks, celestial and human figures are supported on lotus flowers or buds and also stand on the golden land at the bottom; many hold offerings. At the two lower corners a royal figure sits in a walled pavilion attended by female musicians and servants. A Tibetan inscription is written across the bottom praising the abode of "Lord Amitabha," the superiority of his *Dewachen* heaven, and hoping for the rebirth of the "master of painting and all the sentient beings existing under the sky into the best heavenly abode." The mention of Amitabha, Buddha of Boundless Light, here is mysterious although Amitayus can be viewed as one aspect of Amitabha. The back of the *tanka* has a dedication in black Tibetan script written in the form of a *stupa* in the center with vertical lines of red Sanskrit and black Tibetan *mantras* at the sides. The *mantras* are prayers for long life. The dedication says,

> By the merit of making this *tanka*, I wish the sponsor and his family to have a long life and to increase their merit and be saved from demons and evil minded people. Lord Buddha said that a person who does hard work gains patience and that patience is great enlightenment. Also Lord Buddha said that monks who hurt other people or beings or who try to harm another's life are not true monks. To the one who is as red as the *pema ragai* stone and has a smiling face with beautiful watercolored hair flowing down from the right side of his head and who is holding a golden pot which is filled with *amrita* in his *Samadhi mudra* to that deity, Amitayus, I am prostrating. You, the victor, please grant the gift of long life to everyone.

Translations by Nima Dorjee. *Cat. no. 180.*

SAKYA PANDITA

Sakya Pandita (1182-1251) was a great Tibetan scholar and hierarch of the Sakya sect. He and his nephew 'Phags-pa traveled to Mongolia and began the great conversion of that area to Tibetan Buddhism. The saint sits on a Chinese style lacquer throne with dragon finials, tassels and silk coverings. He is dressed in rich gold and red silks and the red hat of the Sakya sect and gestures in a dramatic pose of discourse. Fine offerings are placed before him. At the upper left is Manjusri, from whom all Sakya lamas are believed to descend; at upper right is Lama Grags pa rgyal mtshan, an associate of the Pandita. Mahakala, who assisted the saint in subduing heresy, is at lower left; the Indian sage Harinanda is at lower right. The setting is one of delightful mountains and forests with a monkey family at right and a shrine at left. This *tanka* is part of a series showing the lineage of the Panchen Lama, all of which are finely painted in a pronounced Chinese style. 18th century. *Cat. no. 207.*

GELUGPA ASSEMBLY TREE

This complex gathering of the main deities and saints of the Gelugpa sect is arranged into a central tree with three cloud groups in the sky. Tsong-kha-pa (1357—1419), founder of the Gelugpas, is shown prominently at the apex, wearing the yellow hat of his order and holding an alms-bowl; lotuses extend from each hand supporting a book and a sword; in his heart is Shakyamuni Buddha and in Shak-yamuni's heart is Vajradhara, symbolizing the celestial lineage of Tsong-kha-pa. Below him are Buddhas and saints guarded by fierce deities at top and bottom. The guardians of the four directions, lions, dragons, and precious fruit are at the bottom edge of the tree which grows out of jewel-filled waters. The three cloud groups are dominated by Maitreya (left), Manjusri (right) and Vajradhara (top). Ad-ditional members of the lineage are in four small cloud and two circle groupings. The eight Buddhist emblems, cleverly superimposed, are placed with lotus blossoms at the trunk of the tree. Musicians and Mt. Meru, center of the Universe, are above the waters. At left are objects and figures representing royalty and at right a monk and his assistant present offerings. 19th century. *Cat. no. 209.*

THE WHEEL OF EXISTENCE

This primitively painted *tanka* is a powerful 17th to 18th century example of the endless cycle of rebirth displayed with alarming vividness at the entrance to most Tibetan temples. Devotees were meant to ponder the ultimate delusions of worldly existence while viewing the "wheel" and to be renewed in their striving for release through enlightenment. Clutched by Yama, Lord of Death, the wheel depicts the six realms to which sentient beings are chained, those of the gods (top), titans (upper right), *pretas*, (those guilty of greed in past lives, lower right), hell dwellers (bottom), animals (lower left), and humans (upper left). Each realm has a Buddha who offers salvation with the appropriate symbol in his hands for each realm: "To the gods he brings a lute whose sounds arouse beings from self-complacency; to the titans a sword of wisdom and armor for the spiritual battle; to the *pretas* a vessel containing spiritual food and drink; to the hells a purifying flame; to the animals a book; and to the humans an almsbowl and a pilgrim's staff. The outer rim of the wheel shows the causal nexus or the twelve interdependent causes of rebirth. We may begin at the upper left and proceed clockwise:

1. A blind woman illustrates delusion.
2. A potter illustrates the form-creating activity. As a potter shapes his pots so we shape our karma.
3. A monkey plucking fruit symbolizes consciousness.
4. Two individuals rowing a boat represent personality.
5. An empty house represents the senses.
6. A man and woman embracing symbolizes contact.
7. An arrow entering a man's eye represents feeling.
8. A man being served tea and fine foods symbolizes desire.
9. A person grasping vessels filled with nature's bounty symbolizes clinging to worldly objects.
10. A pregnant woman symbolizes the process of becoming.
11. A newborn child symbolizes birth.
12. A corpse being carried to a cemetery symbolizes death.

Outside of the wheel, in the upper corners, we see Shakyamuni, who taught men how to be free, and Avalokitesvara who helps them to become free.

The Buddha is believed to have formulated his view of life into the "Wheel of Becoming" (*Bhavacakra*) as he meditated under the Tree of Wisdom, and to have first drawn the diagram of the wheel with grains of rice from a stalk which he plucked while walking in a rice field with his disciples. Pictorial details, representing similes and allegories used by Shakyamuni in his teachings, were added to the diagram by the Indian monk Nagarjuna in the second century. Thus the wheel represents one of the oldest Buddhist traditions. The realm of the titans, as well as the Buddhas who stand in each realm, are Tibetan additions. Other details have been adapted to Tibetan life." [1] *Cat. no. 213.*

---

[1] Eleanor Olson, *Catalogue of the Tibetan Collection and other Lamaist Articles*, volume III, pp. 45-6.

A MAHASIDDHA

Mahasiddhas (T. *Grub-thob*), usually
grouped in Tibet in a total of 84, are saints
and miracle workers in control of mystic
forces. As such, they have special importance as symbolic teachers in the esoteric
systems of Buddhism. Although based on
historical or semi-historical persons, the
Mahasiddhas are usually portrayed as cor-
pulent Indian sages, seated on cushions
and an antelope skin (symbolic of their
vow to liberate all suffering beings) with a
cord for assistance in yogic postures
around their chest. The round basket at
left is a container of spiritual food (disci-
pline, teachings and comprehension).
This rare appliqued example is further
distinguished by beautiful garlands of
lotus flowers on the head and body and a
tiny book of scriptures on the piled velvet
hair. The hands form the gesture of teaching. Similar figures have been identified
either as Mahasiddha Virupa or as Pad-ma
mDzad, the lotus eater. It is difficult to determine which of these sages is represented here, as both are associated with
the lotus garland. The figure and his silk
halo and aureole were removed at some
point from their original mounting; it is
probable that he was one of a larger group
sewn to horizontal banners for display in a
large monastery prayer hall. 18th century.
Cat. no. 203.

SAM-YE MONASTERY

Sam-ye, the monastery founded southeast of Lhasa by Padma Sambhava and King Ti-song about 791, was the first of its kind in Tibet. It was modeled after the great Indian monastery of Odantapuri in Bihar. The central gold roofed temple has three stories of mixed Chinese and Indian inspiration, and is surrounded by a cloistered Tibetan style wall with a blue roofed entrance guarded by lions. *Chortens* of different shape and color (red, black, white, and blue) stand at the four quarters along with some smaller shrines and buildings. These are then enclosed by a double zig-zag wall, inside of which various shrines and figures are placed. Gold and red Tibetan lettering identifies most of the structures. Except for the fanciful hill and stream landscape, this painting faithfully represents the main elements of Sam-ye as it looks in photographs taken in the mid-20th century. The 8th century buildings had been destroyed by fire but rebuilt in accordance with the original architecture several times over the centuries. This painting may date from the 17th or 18th centuries. *Cat. no. 212.*

GREEN TARA

The savioress is shown here in her paradise, a fantasy of tiered pavilions, lotus gardens, and angelic musicians. Tara sits in "royal ease" on a lotus petal throne surrounded by radiant light. She holds lotus stems in each hand. Below her are beneficient and ferocious manifestations of the female element. Outside the walls of the palace are charming garlanded trees, nymphs in a lotus pool, a pair of elephants, and monks in caves. The naturalistic placement of the peripheral figures and the treatment of architecture and landscape have been borrowed from Chinese painting but the central focus, Tara, is treated in the hieratic manner traditional in Central Asian and Nepalese painting. This *tanka* is a fine example of the brilliant coloring and decorative embellishments of 18th century Tibetan painting, incorporating several earlier styles into a lyrical visual statement. *Cat. no. 189.*

VAISRAVANA

"The Great Yellow Vaisravana," a form of the god of wealth, is a warrior figure and guardian of the North. He sits in the upper center on a fantastic spotted lion, holding a banner of victory and the mongoose. Surrounding him are eight similarly attired warriors, on ghostly white horses; each holds a mongoose and a weapon or object which identifies him as guardian of one of the eight directions (South, Southwest, West, etc.). These attendants to Vaisravana are the "Eight Masters of the Horses" (T. *rTa bdag brgyad*). In the lower section of the painting eight more war-riors race on horses around a central ninth rider. These are the nine *dgra lha* brothers. Their finely detailed equipment includes red tasseled helmets, tigerskin cases for bows and for arrows, and whips (each followed by a falcon); miniature tigers and lions sit on their shoulders. Demonic figures whirl amongst the brothers, either on foot or on various animal and human mounts. Herds of animals common to Tibet move in from both lower sides toward a central pile of bones and entrails. Below these is a "clothes line" of gargoyle heads alternating with skins of tigers, humans, and an ape (?). Auspicious offerings and weapons are arrayed at the bottom. Vajrapani is situated at the very top of the painting, serving as spiritual mentor to the scene. Paintings on dyed black silk are rare and this *tanka* is an especially effective sample of Tibetan black background demonic visualizations. The transparent style of painting gives the swirling figures an eerie quality. They and their enveloping flame and cloud aureoles appear to vaporize into the dense black environment. 18th century. *Cat. no. 195.*

Catalogue

Nomads of Eastern Tibet

Man with Sword

1. *Chupa*
   deerskin with leopard skin, otter fur, Chinese cotton, satin, silk thread, striped and tie-dyed wool, 60″ l.
   Made in Labrang, Amdo
   Gift of Mrs. C. R. Koenigswald, 1939

2. Hair ornament (shown on modern silk head sash)
   silver with glass beads, 2 1/2 x 3 1/2″ Holton collection, 1936

3. Belt
   ribbed silk with "T" pattern weave, 84″ l.
   Holton collection, 1936

4. Boots
   a&b yak hide and Russian leather with deerskin, striped and tie-dyed wool and Chinese cotton, 22″ h.
   Holton collection, 1936

5. Garters
   a&b striped wool, 46″ l.
   Holton collection, 1936

6. Powder horn and chargers
   two cow horns with wood, leather and antelope horn; six antelope horn chargers with brass and leather, 11 1/4″ l.
   Holton collection, 1936

7. Flint and tinder pouch
   leather with Chinese velvet, silver, brass and steel, 6 1/2 x 3 3/4″
   Crane collection, 1911

8. Sword and scabbard
   a&b steel blade; silver and steel hilt with coral and turquoise; leather and wood sheath with iron and silver; leather waist strap with brass, 35 1/2″ l.
   Crane collection, 1911

9. Matchlock gun
   iron and wood stock with silver wire; leather case and pad with silver; wood fork with antelope horn, brass and silver; iron ramrod, 36 1/2″ l.
   Shelton collection, 1920
   Cat. nos. 1-9 illustrated p. 34.

Man with Gun

10. *Chupa*
    Chinese cotton sateen with sheepskin, silk and otter fur, 60″ l.
    Holton collection, 1936

11. Inner robe
    pulu wool with striped and tie-dyed wool and Chinese cotton, 50″ l.
    Ekvall collection, 1928

12. Hat
    Chinese satin and damask with fox fur and Chinese cotton, 13″ h.
    Holton collection, 1936

13. Braid
    human (?) hair, cotton cord and conch shell, 68″ l.
    Holton collection, 1936

14. Boots
    a&b Russian leather with cow and horse hide, Chinese silk, cotton braid and felt, 18″ h.
    Holton collection, 1936

15. Charmbox
    copper with silver and glass, 5 7/8″ h.
    Shelton collection, 1920

16. Sash
    twill-weave wool, 84″ l.
    Holton collection, 1936

17. Powder pouch
    leather with brass and turquoise, 6 x 10″
    Holton collection, 1936

18. Eating set
    iron knife with brass, copper, horn and bone; iron sheath with copper and brass; wood chopsticks; leather strap, 8 1/2″ l.
    Holton collection, 1936

19. Sword and scabbard
    a&b iron blade; iron hilt with brass and leather; leather and wood sheath with iron, silver, coral and leather, 19 1/4″ l.
    Made at Derge
    Crane collection, 1911

20. Matchlock gun
    iron barrel; wood stock with bone, brass and silver; leather case and pad with silver, antelope horn and wood fork; leather carrying strap, 62″ l.
    Crane collection, 1911
    Cat. nos. 10-20 illustrated p. 32.

Woman

21. *Chupa*
    Chinese satin brocade with silk damask, cotton and otter fur, 55″ l.
    Holton collection, 1936

22. Inner robe
    Chinese cotton sateen with sheepskin and otter fur, 57″ l.
    Holton collection, 1936

23. Jacket
    Chinese silk brocade with cotton, lambskin and otter fur, 25″ l.
    Ekvall collection, 1928

24. Sash
    Chinese raw silk, 192″ l.
    Holton collection, 1936

25. Headdress
    padded wool with Chinese silk, silk fringe, velvet and cotton; attached silver discs with coral, glass and amber; attached Chinese silver coins; yak hair and twine wig, 60″ l.
    Holton collection, 1936

26. Hat
    Chinese cotton with felt and lambskin, 11″ h.
    Holton collection, 1936

27. Boots
    a&b Russian leather with cow and horse hide, velvet, cotton and felt, 17″ h.
    Holton collection, 1936

28. Chatelaine
    leather and Chinese brocade with printed cotton and cotton cord; silver and gold plaque with turquoise, 13″ l.; hinged silver pendant from which hangs a Chinese silk tassel and an eating set of fine Chinese workmanship: steel knife with wood handle, silver and turquoise; wood sheath with silver, turquoise, coral, lapis lazuli, garnet, agate and glass; ivory chopsticks, 8 1/2″ l.
    Holton collection, 1936
    Cat. nos. 21-28 illustrated p. 29.

29. Charmbox
    silver with copper and glass, 5″ d.
    Holton collection, 1936

Child

30. *Chupa*
    Chinese cotton with lambskin, striped and tie-dyed wool and damask, 27″ l.
    Ekvall collection, 1928

31. Shirt
    Chinese cotton damask, 16 3/4″ l.
    Crane collection, 1911

32. Sash
    Chinese cotton, 69″ l.
    Holton collection, 1936

33. Hat
    Chinese velvet with damask, felt and fox fur, 12″ h.
    Gift of Mrs. C. R. Koenigswald, 1939

34. Charmbox
    silver with silver filigree, coral, turquoise and copper, 5 1/2″ d.
    Holton collection, 1936
    Illustrated p. 36.

35. Man's hair ornament
    silver with imitation coral and copper, 4″ w.
    Holton collection, 1936

36. Woman's hair ornament
    silver with coral, turquoise and copper, 4 1/2″ w.
    Gift of Schuyler Cammann, 1941
    Cat. nos. 35 and 36 illustrated p. 30.

37. Milk pail hook
    brass, attached silver medallions with turquoise and glass; leather strap, 6 1/4″ l.
    Holton collection, 1936
    Illustrated p. 26

38. Pair of woman's belt pendants
    a&b silver with coral, malachite, turquoise and glass, 28 1/2″ l.
    Service collection, 1948

39. Pair of woman's earrings
    a&b silver with imitation coral and turquoise, 2 1/2″ l.
    Crane collection, 1911

40. Pair of woman's earrings
    a&b silver with glass, 4 1/2″ l.
    Holton collection, 1936

41. Woman's hair ornament
    copper with silver wire, turquoise and brass, 2″ d.
    Holton collection, 1936

42. Man's pendant earring
silver with imitation coral, coral and turquoise, 3⁷/₈″ l.
Holton collection, 1936

43. Ring
silver with turquoise, ⁷/₈″ l.
Crane collection, 1911

44. Ring
silver with turquoise, ³/₄″ l.
Holton collection, 1936

45. Saddle ring
silver with coral, 1⁷/₈″ l.
Holton collection, 1936
Cat. nos. 39-45 illustrated p. 31.

46. Sword and scabbard
a&b iron blade; iron hilt with silver wire and
turquoise; leather-covered wood scabbard
with iron, silver, turquoise and coral,
32¹/₄″ l.
Holton collection, 1936
Illustrated p. 35.

47. Quiver
a-e wood with wool, leather, silver, brass and
iron; leather strap, 34″ l.; five bamboo
arrows with feathers and iron points,
31″ l.
Shelton collection, 1920

48. Whistling arrow
bamboo shaft with feathers and wood
head, 36″ l.
Shelton collection, 1920
Cat. nos. 47 a-e and 48 illustrated p. 28.

49. Whip
antelope horn handle with silver, copper
and leather; braided leather strap; iron
loops, 45¹/₂″ l.
Ekvall collection, 1928

50. Teapot
wood burl with brass, copper and twine,
12¹/₂″ h.
Service collection, 1948
Illustrated p. 37.

51. Pitcher
wood burl with brass and copper, 7¹/₂″ h.
Service collection, 1948

52. Covered pail
a&b copper with brass; iron handle, 13¹/₂″ h.
Service collection, 1948
Illustrated p. 27.

53. Canteen
iron with silver damascene and brass; iron
lid with brass and leather; iron loops;
leather strap, 15″ h.
Made in Chamdo
Shelton collection, 1920

54. Butter jar
a&b wood with brass, 7″ h.
Holton collection, 1936

55. Tea and butter churn
a&b wood willow loops; wood dasher, 26″ h.
Shelton collection, 1914

56. Flint and tinder pouch
leather with brass, copper, silver, coral
and steel; leather strap with mother of
pearl button, 4³/₄″ l.
Ekvall collection, 1928

57. Snuff horn
a&b yak horn with silver, coral and turquoise;
wood stopper with silver; silk tassel,
11″ l.
Holton collection, 1936

58. Snuff bottle
a&b wood burl with silver and glass; silver
stopper and copper spoon; leather strap,
5¹/₂″ l.
Holton collection, 1936
*Cat. nos. 57 a & b and 58 a & b illustrated
p. 33.*

59. Snuff horn
a&b horn with silver; wood stopper with bone;
leather strap, 10¹/₂″ l.
Crane collection, 1911

60. Box and dice
a-f three wood dice with horn (?); Chinese tin
box; wool case with Chinese cotton, copper and leather, 3″ d.
Holton collection, 1936

61. Belt
Chinese cotton, 96 x 4¹/₂″
Woven by the Chiang and Chiarong tribes
in the Chinese-Tibetan borderlands
Holton collection, 1936

62. Felt rug
wool with over-laid wool fiber design, 72 x
4¹/₂″
Probably of Mongol manufacture
Holton collection, 1936

63. Blanket
wool with tie-dyed design, 45 x 26″
Purchase 1929

Note: All objects described in this section are
from Amdo or Kham and date from the 19th to
the early 20th centuries unless otherwise noted.

The Lhasa Nobility

64. Appliqued tent for summer outings
Indian cotton with appliqued Indian cotton and Tibetan wool designs; Indian
printed cotton lining; yak hair ropes covered in Indian cotton and dyed yak hair
pompoms, 120 x 180″ (Originally set up
with bamboo ridge pole and two support
poles stabilized by ropes. Sides hook onto
roof with iron s-hooks.) Made in Sikkim in
the 1930's by a Lhasa tentmaker.
Purchase 1959, Thomas L. Raymond
Bequest Fund
Illustrated pp. 42-43.

65. Prayer flags
a-d Indian cotton with printed designs, sewn
onto cord, (4 sets) 9 to 24″ l.
Purchase 1947 and Gift of Dr. S. Ernest
Sussman, 1961

Official's Summer Costume

66. *Chupa*
Chinese silk brocade with satin damask,
printed Indian cotton; gold button,
61¹/₂″ l.
Tsepon Shakabpa collection, 1972
Purchase 1972, C. Suydam Cutting
Endowment Fund

67. Hat
Chinese silk brocade with damask and silk
fringe; Chinese silk streamers with silk
cord and silk floss, 13¹/₄″ d. (finial, cat.
no. 69 attaches at top)
Purchase 1974, C. Suydam Cutting
Bequest Fund

68. Boots
a&b leather with Chinese silk damask, cotton
braid and wool, 14″ h.
Purchase 1974, C. Suydam Cutting
Bequest Fund
Cat. nos. 66-68 a & b illustrated p. 44.

69. Official's hat finial (T. *Shalok*)
gold filigree with orange wash, seed
pearls, glass, turquoise and silver,
3¹/₂″ h. (attaches to top of hat, cat. no. 67)
Made in Lhasa, Tsepon Shakabpa
collection
Purchase 1972, C. Suydam Cutting
Endowment Fund
Illustrated p. 45.

Official's Ceremonial Robe

70. *Chupa*
Russian brocade with silk cord, beaver (?)
fur trim; Chinese silk damask lining;
brass button, 52″ l.
Sonam Topjor Tethong collection
Purchase 1977, Sophronia Anderson
Bequest Fund

71. Collar
Russian brocade with silk cord, velvet and
Chinese silk damask; brass button,
15³/₈″ l.
Sonam Topjor Tethong collection
Purchase 1977, Sophronia Anderson
Bequest Fund

72. Outer collar
otter (?) fur with Chinese cotton and silk
damask; brass button, 16³/₈″ l.
Sonam Topjor Tethong collection
Purchase 1977, Sophronia Anderson
Bequest Fund

73. Sash
Persian brocade, silver fringe and Euro-
pean (?) silk damask, 107³/₈″ l.
Sonam Topjor Tethong collection
Purchase 1977, Sophronia Anderson
Bequest Fund
Cat. nos. 70-73 illustrated p. 47.

Noble Woman

74. *Chupa*
Chinese satin with cut velvet, Chinese silk
damask and Indian printed cotton; gold
button, 58⁷/₈″ l.
Collection of the Dalai Lama's elder sister
Purchase 1971, C. Suydam Cutting
Endowment Fund

75. Apron
pulu wool with Indian silk brocade and
Indian printed cotton, 27³/₄″ l.
Purchase 1961

76. Headdress (replica)
cotton with turquoise and imitation pearl,
coral and turquoise, 13″ l.; human hair
wig on cloth and metal support; silk
tassels, 60″ l.
Purchase 1973, John J. O'Neill Bequest
Fund

77. Pair of earrings
a&b brass with turquoise, pearl and coral,
4³/₈″ l.
Gift 1959, Eleanor Olson

78. Charmbox
silver alloy with gold foil and turquoise;
strung on necklace of coral, turquoise and
glass, 4″ sq.
Purchase 1974, C. Suydam Cutting
Bequest Fund

79. Necklace
coral and imitation amber; mother of
pearl and coral breast ornament; attached
gilt copper plaques with turquoise and
glass; silver hooks with turquoise, 17″ l.
Purchase 1973, Felix Fuld Bequest Fund

80. Boots
a&b embroidered cotton, 15″ h.
Chinese manufacture
Holton collection, 1936
Cat. nos. 74-80 illustrated p. 48.

Seated Woman

81. *Chupa*
Chinese silk damask with Indian cotton;
gold button, 48¹/₂″ l.
Purchase 1956

82. Blouse
Chinese silk damask, 20³/₈″ l.
Purchase 1973, Mrs. C. Suydam Cutting
Endowment Fund

83. Apron
pulu wool with Indian brocade and Indian cotton; silk braided ties, 27¹/₂″ l.
Purchase 1956

84. Official's earrings
a&b gold with turquoise, gold and glass; Chi-
nese silk tape, 6¹/₈″ l.; pearl and tur-
quoise strung on wool cord, 1¹/₂″ l.
Made in Lhasa
Tashi Tshering collection
Purchase 1961, C. Suydam Cutting
Endowment Fund
Illustrated p. 46.

85. Pair of woman's earrings
a&b silver with turquoise, 3¹/₂″ l.
Purchase 1948, Alice E. Getty collection

86. Man's earring
silver with turquoise, 1⁵/₈″ l.
Purchase 1962

87. Bracelet
silver with turquoise, 2¹/₄″ d.
Purchase 1943
Cat. nos. 86 and 87 illustrated p. 46.

88. Seals and wax
two iron, one brass, and one iron and brass
seal, attached by cord to a lump of sealing
wax; seals: 1¹/₄″−2¹/₄″ l.
Crane collection, 1911
Illustrated p. 49.

89. Official's seal
wood, 2³/₄″ l.
Holton collection, 1936

90. Pen case
iron with traces of gilt, 15³/₈″ l.
Made in Derge
Shelton collection, 1920
Illustrated p. 49.

91. Ink pot
a&b copper with brass, 3¹/₄″ h.
Holton collection, 1936

92. Coffer
copper, partially gilded with glass and tur-
quoise, 11¹/₄ x 16³/₄″
Purchase 1963, C. Suydam Cutting
Endowment Fund
Illustrated p. 50.

93. Folding table
brass and copper, 11¹/₄ x 19¹/₂″
Purchase 1952

94. Beer jug
iron with gold and silver damascene and
brass, 15¹/₄″ h.
Chamdo, Eastern Tibet
Shelton collection, 1920
Illustrated p. 52.

95. Tea pot
a&b copper and brass, 10¹/₂″ h.
Made in Derge, Eastern Tibet
Crane collection, 1911

96. Covered tea bowl
Indian (?) ivory with silver, coral and tur-
quoise; silver lid with coral, 4⁵/₈″ h.
Purchase 1972, C. Suydam Cutting
Endowment Fund
Illustrated p. 53.

97. Cup in traveling container
a&b Chinese porcelain with enamel design;
mark of Kuang hsü (1875-1908); wool
case with leather and brass, 5¹/₂″ d.
Amdo
Purchase 1928

98. Basket
straw with cloth tab, 6″ d.
Made in Bhutan
Tsepon Shakabpa collection
Gift 1972

99. Headdress case
painted wood with brass; Indian silk
lining, 22″ l.
(for wig and headdress, cat. no. 76)
Made in Lhasa
Tsepon Shakabpa collection
Purchase 1973, John J. O'Neill Bequest
Fund

100. Rug
wool pile, cotton warp and weft,
29³/₄ x 31³/₈″
Chinese manufacture
Gift of Susan D. Bliss, 1966

101. Blanket
wool with tie-dyed design, 32 x 26″
Purchase 1929

102. Saddle
wood with leather and silver, 22 x 14¹/₂″
Shelton collection, 1920

103. Stirrups and crupper
cast iron stirrups with gold damascene,
wood, leather and iron; leather crupper
with gold and silver damascened iron and
silver, 29³/₄″ l.; 26¹/₈″ l.
Shelton collection, 1920

104. Saddle pad
Chinese silk damask with cotton, leather
and silver and gold damascened iron,
15¹/₂″ l.
Shelton collection, 1920

105. Saddle blanket
wool and velvet, silk cord and fringe,
cotton and gilt leather, 56″ l.
Shelton collection, 1920
Cat. nos. 102-105 illustrated p. 51.

106. *Tamka* coin
silver, 1¹/₁₆″ d.
Minted at Lhasa, 18th (?) century
Crane collection, 1911

107. Tibeto-Nepalese *tamka* coin
silver alloy, 1″ d.
Minted in Nepal, 1722
Crane collection, 1911

108. Tibeto-Chinese *tamka* coin
silver, 1¹/₁₆″ d.
Minted at Lhasa, ca. 1821-50
Crane collection, 1911

109. 100 *srang* note
paper, 5¹/₂ x 8¹/₂″
Printed in Lhasa, 1945-50
Gift of Thubten T. Liushar, 1964

110. 50 *tamka* note
paper, 4⁵/₈ x 7⁷/₈″
Printed in Lhasa, 1929
Gift of Thubten T. Liushar, 1964

Note: All objects described in this section were
made in Tibet and date from the 19th and 20th
centuries unless otherwise noted.

Ritual and Ceremony

111. Prayer wheel
brass with copper, shell, turquoise, coral
and brass; lacquered bamboo handle with
brass, 10³/₈″ l.
Purchase 1971, C. Suydam Cutting Endowment Fund

112. Rosary
yellow glass, agate, amber and imitation
amber beads divided into six sections by
dyed agate beads, silver discs and counters
with coral and turquoise; leather string,
33″ l.
Holton Collection, 1936
Cat. nos. 111 and 112 illustrated p. 66.

113. Rosary
108 human (?) skull bone discs with turquoise, coral and lapis lazuli, divided into
four sections by turquoise, lapis lazuli,
wood and coral beads; silver counters; silk
cord, 16¹/₄″ l.
Gift of Alice Boney, 1956

114. Charmbox
copper with silver and gilt silver, 7¹/₄″ h.
Gift of Paul E. Manheim, 1968
Illustrated p. 62.

115. Offering scarf (T. *kata*)
Chinese satin damask woven with Tibetan
inscription; silk fringe, 50″ l.
Gift of Eleanor Olson, 1963

116. Two molds for votive images (T. *ts'a ts'a*)
a-d copper and iron, 1$\frac{7}{8}$" l.; (recessed mold for image of seated Bodhisattva) brass, 3$\frac{1}{2}$" l.; (recessed mold for image of *chorten* with Tibetan inscription)
Crane collection, 1911

117. Mold for dough effigies
wood with incised images, 14" l.
Purchase 1971, C. Suydam Cutting Endowment Fund
Illustrated p. 63.

118. Set of cards
a-e three: polychrome paint on paper, 4$\frac{3}{4}$" h., two: polychrome paint on cotton, 4" h.
Shelton collection, 1920

119. *Mani* stone
carved and painted shale, 8$\frac{1}{2}$ x 13$\frac{1}{2}$"
Kham
Purchase 1930
Illustrated p. 63.

120. Table
carved and painted wood, 11$\frac{1}{8}$" h.
Purchase 1975, Felix Fuld Bequest Fund

121. Altar cloth
Chinese satin brocade with cotton lining, 64" l.
Collection of the Prince of Batang, Kham
Shelton collection, 1920

122. Two butter lamps
a & b silver, 9$\frac{1}{2}$" h.; Tibetan inscription on bases
Shelton collection, 1920

123. Large butter lamp
silver, 13$\frac{3}{4}$" h.; Tibetan inscription on base
Shelton collection, 1920
Illustrated p. 60.

124. Set of four butter lamps
a-d silver, 4$\frac{3}{4}$" - 5$\frac{1}{4}$" h.; Tibetan inscription on bases
Shelton collection, 1920

125. Ceremonial plate
copper and silver-plated copper, 15$\frac{1}{4}$" d.
Outer Mongolia
Purchase 1929

126. Pair of offering bowls
a&b silver, 6$\frac{1}{2}$" d.; Tibetan inscriptions
Shelton collection, 1920

127. Pair of censors
a&b silver, 37" h.
Shelton collection, 1920

128. Holy water vase
a&b a. copper with silver and brass rim; Chinese cotton "gown," 5$\frac{1}{2}$" h.
Holton collection, 1936

Aspergillum
b. black feathers and peacock feathers with silk cord and jade ring, 15$\frac{3}{4}$" h.
Probably from China
Gift of Lois Clark, 1973

129. Holy water vase
silver, 7" h.
Shelton collection, 1920

130. Basin on tripod
a&b silver with turquoise, 5$\frac{1}{2}$" h.
Shelton collection, 1920

131. Covered bowl
a&b silver, 3$\frac{1}{2}$" d.
Crane collection, 1911

132. Skull-cup
silver, 3" h.
Crane collection, 1911

133. Stepped *mandala*
a-e silver with turquoise and coral, 5$\frac{3}{4}$" d.
Purchase 1972, Mathilde Oestrich Bequest Fund

134. Wheel of the law
silver, 20$\frac{1}{4}$" h.
Crane collection, 1911
Illustrated p. 65.

135. Miniature *chorten*
cast bronze, traces of gilding, glass chips, 7$\frac{5}{8}$" h.
Crane collection, 1911
Illustrated p. 72.

136. Pair of banners
a&b appliqued Chinese silk brocade with silk cord; Chinese silk brocade streamers with silk floss tassels and cotton, 238$\frac{1}{8}$" l.
Purchase 1974, C. Suydam Cutting Bequest Fund
Cat. no. 136a illustrated p. 64.

137. Pair of *makura* finials
a&b brass with copper, 9$\frac{1}{2}$" h.
Service collection, 1948

138. Pair of rugs
a&b cotton warp and weft, 106" h.
Woven in Ninghsia, China (?) for Tibetan or Mongolian use
Gift of Henry H. Wehrhane, 1942
Cat. nos. 137 and 138a illustrated p. 61.

139. Cape
wool pile, wool warp and weft with tie-dyed wool; lined with cotton stamped "made in Italy," 64" l.
Holton collection, 1936

140. Ceremonial robe
Chinese satin damask formed of 125 rectangular patches with silk thread and embroidered satin, 53 x 120"
Acquired from the Ba Lama, Batang
Crane collection, 1911

141. Crested hat
cotton with wool pile and wool thread; Chinese silk lappets and fringe, 26" l.
Holton collection, 1936

142. Mitre shaped hat
wool with cotton, 15" h.
Holton collection, 1936

143. Abbot's hat
lacquered wool with silk and cotton, 14$\frac{1}{2}$" d.
Purchase 1975, Nathaniel Kent Fund
Cat. nos. 141-143 illustrated p. 77.

Dance Costume
144. Gown
Chinese silk brocade with satin; brass button, 53" l.
Gift of Alice Boney, 1954

145. Collar
Chinese brocade with satin and cotton; brass button, 33" sq.
From the collection of the Ba Lama, Batang
Crane collection, 1911

146. Mask
painted papier-mâché with wire, glass and cotton, 22" h.
Obtained in Peking in 1903
Acquired by exchange with the American Museum of Natural History, 1948
Cat. nos. 144-146 illustrated p. 67.

147. Mask
carved and painted wood, 19" h.
Gift of Charles R. Scott, 1923
Illustrated p. 70.

148. Canopy
silk with 300 embroidered "peacock feathers," 62" l.
Chinese embroidery (?) assembled in Tibet
Gift of Mrs. Thyra H. Maxwell in memory of Miss Grace Nicholson, 1952

149. Dancer's apron
Chinese silk appliqued with silk and gilt leather; embroidery and silk fringe, 33" l.
Purchase 1969, Harry E. Sautter Endowment Fund
Illustrated p. 68.

150. Saddle cloth and cover
a&b cloth: cotton with appliqued silk and gilt leather, painted details, 59" l.
cover: Chinese silk damask with appliqued silk and gilt leather, 25" w.
Purchase 1918
Illustrated p. 69.

151. Decree of the Peking Lama
ink and colors on satin, 108$\frac{1}{2}$" l.
Shelton collection, 1918
Illustrated p. 71.

152. Letter and envelope from the 13th Dalai Lama
ink on paper with seal, 23$\frac{3}{8}$" h.
(dated in accordance with October 14, 1933)
Gift of Mrs. C. Suydam Cutting, 1973

153. Letter from the 14 Dalai Lama
ink on paper with seal, 27" h.
(dated in accordance with October 22, 1948)
Gift of Mrs. C. Suydam Cutting, 1973

154. *Dorje* and bell
a&b *dorje*: brass, 6$\frac{5}{8}$" l.
bell: bronze with brass handle and iron clapper, 9$\frac{1}{2}$" h.
Made in Nepal (?)
Shelton collection, 1920
Illustrated p. 72.

155. Astrological handbook
75 paper folios, woodblock printed with hand coloring; applied and moveable discs and pointers; stitched Chinese silk damask cover, 10$\frac{3}{4}$ x 3$\frac{7}{8}$"
Holton collection, 1936

156. Chopper
iron, 11$\frac{1}{2}$" h.
Purchase 1954

157. *Phur-pa* ("stake" or "peg")
carved and painted wood, 16¼" l.
Holton collection, 1936
Cat. nos. 156 and 157 illustrated p. 74.

158. Whisk
yak tail, 24" l.
Holton collection, 1936

159. Libation ewer
silver with gold wash, 12½" h.
Shelton collection, 1920
Illustrated p. 73.

160. Teapot
silver with gold wash, 14" h.
Shelton collection, 1920
Illustrated p. 76.

161. Bowl and stand
a&b jade and silver, 6¼" h.
Shelton collection, 1920
Illustrated p. 75.

162. Pair of bowls
a&b wood burl with silver, 7" d., 2⅞" d.
Crane collection, 1911

163. Large drum with beater
a&b carved and painted wood with leather;
wood handle with leather and iron,
16" d.; wood beater, 21½" l.
Gift of Eleanor Olson, 1973
Illustrated p. 79.

164. Skull drum
skull-cup with wood, leather and wool;
leather clappers; embroidered silk streamers, 5¼" d.
Crane collection, 1911

165. Small rattle drum
ivory with silver, turquoise and leather;
cotton cord clappers; Indian silk streamer,
3⅜" d.
Purchase 1972, Mathilde Oestrich
Bequest Fund
Cat. nos. 164 and 165 illustrated p. 81.

166. Large rattle drum
wood with leather and wool; cotton cord
clappers; silk streamer with imitation
amber and shell, 7⅝" d.
Purchase 1962

167. Pair of telescopic trumpets
a&b copper with brass, 97½" l.
Service collection, 1948

168. Pair of trumpets
a&b copper with brass, copper wire and glass,
15¾" l.
Shelton collection, 1920

169. Pair of telescopic trumpets
a&b brass with copper, 56" l.
Shelton collection, 1920

170. Horn
welk horn with brass and copper, 11¾" l.
Shelton collection, 1920

171. Pair of dragon trumpets
a&b silver with copper, 17½" l.
Shelton collection, 1920

172. Serpentine trumpet
antelope horn with silver, turquoise and
coral, 21¾" l.
Purchase 1972, Mathilde Oestrich
Bequest Fund

173. Pair of trumpets
a&b silver with turquoise and coral; silk floss
tassels, 16½" l.
Gift of Eleanor Olson, 1974
Cat. nos. 170-173 illustrated p. 80.

174. Trumpet
human thigh bone with silver and brass
wire, silver plated copper set with glass
and leather, 13¼" l.
Crane collection, 1911

175. Pair of large cymbals
a&b bronze with leather handles, 14" d.
Shelton collection, 1920

176. Small cymbals
bronze with brass chain and leather
thongs, 3" d.
Crane collection, 1911
*Cat. nos. 175 a & b and 176 illustrated
p. 81.*

Note: All objects described in this section were
made in Tibet and date from the 18th through
the early 20th centuries unless otherwise noted.
Names of deities are given in their most common Sanskrit or Tibetan form. Tibetan (T.)
transliterated names are provided when
appropriate.

The Spiritual World

177. Vajrasattva (T. *rDo-rje Sems-dpah*)
hollow cast bronze with copper, silver,
pitch (?), turquoise
and coral, 17⅞" h.
15th-16th century
Purchase 1973, The Members' Fund
Illustrated p. 98.

178. Vajradhara (T. *rDo-rje hChang*)
hollow cast copper, gilded with turquoise
and coral stones;
painted details, 18¾" h.
17th century
Purchase 1970, The Members' Fund
Illustrated p. 89.

179. Crowned Buddha
hollow cast bronze, gilded, 18½" h.
Made in China during the Ming Period
(1368-1644)
Herman and Paul Jaehne collection, 1941
Illustrated p. 93.

180. Paradise of Amitayus (T. *Tshe-dpag-med*)
colors and gold on cotton, 33⅝ x 29⅝"
Late 16th-early 17th century
Purchase 1976, Sophronia Anderson
Bequest Fund, Membership Endowment
Fund and Charles W. Engelhard Bequest
Fund
Illustrated p. 110.

181. Book cover
carved wood, gilded; painted details,
28 x 10½"
16th-17th century
Purchase 1977, Members' Contribution
for Paris Trip
Illustrated p. 90.

182. Two folios from volumes of the *Kanjur* (T.
a&b *bKa'-gyur*)
ink, colors and gold on paper, 8 x 25½"
Crane collection, 1911

183. A volume of the *Kanjur* (T. *bKa'-gyur*)
a-c 346 paper folios with ink, colors and gold,
8¾ x 27"; 2 carved, painted and gilded
wood covers, 9" x 28½"
ca. 16th-17th century
Shelton collection, 1920
Illustrated p. 91.

184. *Mandala* of Akshobhya Buddha (T. *Mi
hKhrug-pa*)
colors on cotton, 36" sq.
19th century
Shelton collection, 1920

185. A Bodhisattva
a&b solid cast bronze, gilded, 18" h.
17th-18th century
Gift of C. Suydam Cutting, 1950
Illustrated p. 104.

186. Avalokitesvara (T. *sPyan-ras-gzigs Phyag-
bZhi-pa*)
applied Chinese silk with embroidered details; applied glass beads, 54½ x 33½"
18th century
Purchase 1957, Mr. C. Suydam Cutting
and Mrs. C. Suydam Cutting Endowment
Funds
Illustrated p. 92.

187. Devi ("goddess")
solid cast copper, traces of gilt, 8⅛" h.
15th-16th century
Purchase 1970, The Members' Fund
Illustrated p. 94.

188. Tara (T. *Sgrol-ma*)
a&b solid cast copper, gilded with turquoise
stones; jewelry; repoussé copper base and
mandorla, gilded, 28" h.
Made in Nepal 17th century
Shelton collection, 1920
Illustrated p. 88.

189. Green tara (T. *sGrol-ljang*)
colors and gold on cotton, 34¼ x 21"
18th century
Purchase 1969, Felix Fuld Bequest Fund
Illustrated p. 119.

190. *Mandala* of Vasudhara (T. *Nor-rGyun-ma*)
gold on paper, 34" sq.
18th-19th century
Gift of Mrs. Frank L. Babbott, 1954
Illustrated p. 95.

191. *Mandala* of the Fierce and Tranquil
Deities (T. *Zhi-khro dKyil-'khor*)
colors and gold on cotton, 28½ x 19"
17th-18th century
Purchase 1969, The Members' Fund
Illustrated p. 96.

192. Dharmapala (T. *Chos-skyong*)
solid cast bronze; painted details,
11¼" h.
12th-13th century
Shelton collection, 1920
Illustrated p. 97.

193. Vajrapani (T. *Phyag-na rDo-rje*)
solid cast copper gilded, 8" h.
17th-18th century
Gift of Doris Wiener, 1969
Illustrated p. 99.

194. Bse'i Khrab Can ("He who has a cuirass of
     leather")
     ink, colors and gold on cotton, 42 x 31"
     19th century
     Shelton collection, 1920
     Illustrated p. 100.

195. Vaisravana (T. *rNam sras ser chen*)
     colors on silk, 31³/₈ x 23¹/₈"
     18th century
     Purchase 1972, The Members' Fund
     Illustrated p. 120.

196. Jambhala and Vasudhara
     solid cast copper, gilded; painted details,
     8¹/₂" h.
     17th century
     Shelton collection, 1920

197. Woodblock
     carved wood, 8³/₄ x 21¹/₂"
     18th century
     Purchase 1940

198. Dorje Phur-pa
     solid cast bronze, 10³/₄" h.
     ca. 13th century
     Gift of Mr. and Mrs. Jack Zimmerman in
     honor of Eleanor Olson, 1970
     Illustrated p. 101.

199. Vajravarahi (T. *rDo-rje Phag-mo*)
     solid cast silver, gilded and painted details
     with turquoise stones, 15" h.
     17th-18th century
     Purchase 1970, Mary Livingston Griggs
     and Mary Griggs Burke Foundation
     Illustrated p. 102.

200. Padma Sambhava (T. *Gu-ru rin-po-che*)
     hollow cast bronze with traces of poly-
     chrome, 6¹/₄" h.
     15th-16th century
     Gift of Nasli Heeramaneck, 1970
     Illustrated p. 103.

201. Paradise of Padma Sambhava
     colors and gold on cotton, 24¹/₄ x 16¹/₄"
     17th century
     Purchase, 1969, The Members' Fund
     Illustrated p. 105.

202. Guru Drag-po-che and his retinue
     colors and gold on cotton, 31 x 25"
     17th century
     Crane collection, 1911

203. A Mahasiddha (T. *Grub-thob*)
     appliqued Chinese silk with embroidered
     details, 50⁵/₈ x 38⁷/₈"
     18th century
     Purchase 1976, Wallace M. Scudder
     Bequest Fund and The Members' Fund
     Illustrated p. 117.

204. Milarepa
     hollow cast bronze with silver, glass, lapis
     lazuli and turquoise stones, 4³/₈" h.
     ca. 15th century
     Purchase 1975, Sophronia Anderson
     Bequest Fund
     Illustrated p. 106.

205. Two folios from the *Biography of*
a&b *Milarepa*
     ink and colors on paper, 4 x 23"
     17th-18th century
     Holton collection, 1936
     Illustrated p. 109.

206. Pair of portrait images
a&b carved and painted wood, 15³/₄" h.;
     15¹/₄" h.
     19th (?) century
     Purchase 1975, The Members' Fund
     Illustrated p. 107.

207. Sakya Pandita
     colors and gold on cotton, 24¹/₂ x 14"
     18th century
     Purchase 1969, Felix Fuld Bequest Fund
     Illustrated p. 112.

208. Lama Gyawa Rgod-Tshang-Pa Mgon-Po
     Rdorje
     hollow cast with copper and silver;
     painted details, 26" h.
     16th century
     Purchase 1969, The Members' Fund
     Illustrated p. 108.

209. Gelugpa Assembly Tree
     colors and gold on cotton, 30 x 21"
     19th century
     Shelton collection, 1920
     Illustrated p. 113.

210. The Seventh Dalai Lama
     colors and gold on cotton, 23¹/₄ x 16¹/₂"
     19th century
     Shelton collection, 1920

211. Monk
     Hollow cast bronze, gilded, 9⁷/₈" h.
     16th-17th century
     Herman and Paul Jaehne collection, 1941

212. Sam-ye Monastery (T. *bSam-yas dGon-pa*)
     colors and gold on cotton, 21 x 15"
     17th-18th century
     Shelton collection, 1920
     Illustrated p. 118.

213. The Wheel of Existence (T. *Srid-pahi
     hKhor-lo*)
     colors on cotton, 43 x 34"
     17th-18th century
     Purchase 1936
     Illustrated p. 115.

Note: All objects described in this section were
made in Tibet unless otherwise noted. Names
of deities are given in their most common
Sanskrit or Tibetan form. Tibetan (T.) transliterated names are provided when appropriate.

Glossary of Symbols

Some common symbols, derived from Indian and Chinese mythology, used on ritual and domestic objects in Tibet are listed below:

The All-Powerful Ten, a mystic monogram composed of ten Sanskrit letters, emblem of the *Kalachakra* cycle of time doctrines.

Dragon, a celestial guardian with magical powers over water as well as symbol of the Chinese nation and emperor.

Eight Buddhist Emblems, umbrella (royalty), twin fish (freedom from restraint), conch shell (the spoken word, power over water), lotus (divine birth and purity), wheel (the word set in motion), standard of victory (attainment of enlightenment), vase (container of holy water or treasures), and endless knot (longevity).

Garuda, part bird, part human conqueror of serpents, guardian of the sky.

Lotus, see Eight Buddhist Emblems.

Makura, a mythological sea monster, serving as a protective spirit.

Monster Mask (T. *Chi-mi 'dra*), originating from the Chinese *T'ao-t'ieh* and the Indian *Kirtimukha*, both giving forth snakes or jewels from a disembodied head, symbolic of the wealth and delusions of the world; used in Tibet as an emblem of protection.

Shou, Chinese character for longevity.

Swastika, symbol of endless moving.

The Three Jewels, represent the triad of Buddha, *Dharma* (law) and *Sangha* (congregation).

Whirling Emblem, symbol of ceaseless change.

Yin-yang Emblem, represents universal dualism.

Bibliography

Carrasco, *Land and Polity in Tibet*, Seattle: University of Washington Press, 1959.

Ekvall, Robert B., *Religious Observances in Tibet: Patterns and Function*, Chicago: University of Chicago Press, 1964.

Evans-Wentz, W. Y., *Tibet's Great Yogi Milarepa*, Oxford, 1928.

Hoffman, Helmut, *The Religions of Tibet*, New York: MacMillan, 1961.

Hoffman, Helmut, *Tibet, A Handbook*, Bloomington: Indiana University Asian Studies Research Institute, 1973.

Norbu, Thubten Jigme and Colin M. Turnbull, *Tibet*, New York: Simon and Schuster, 1968.

Olschak, Blanche C. and Geshe Thupten Wangyal, *Mystic Art of Ancient Tibet*, New York: McGraw-Hill, 1973.

Olson, Eleanor, *Catalogue of the Tibetan Collections and Other Lamaist Articles in the Newark Museum*, 5 volumes, Newark, 1950-70.

Pal Pratapaditya, *The Art of Tibet*, New York: The Asia Society, 1969.

Shakabpa, Tsepon W. D. *Tibet, A Political History*, New Haven: Yale University Press, 1967.

Snellgrove, David and Hugh Richardson, *A Cultural History of Tibet*, New York: Praeger, 1968.

Stein, R. A., *Tibetan Civilization*, London: Faber and Faber, 1962.

Taring, Rinchen Dolma, *Daughter of Tibet*, London: John Murray, 1970.

Tucci, Guiseppe, *Tibetan Painted Scrolls*, 3 volumes, Rome: La Libreria Dello Stato, 1946.

Photo Credits